The Original
Liverpool Sound

Published by Liverpool University Press
4 Cambridge Street
Liverpool L69 7ZU

Copyright © 2009 Royal Liverpool Philharmonic

Book design by March Graphic Design Studio, Liverpool
Printed and bound by Gutenberg Press, Malta

Commissioned photography by Mark McNulty. With grateful thanks for
wonderful photographic contributions from Jon Barraclough, Terry and Paul
Mealey, Rogan MacDonald, Chris Thomond, Leila Romaya, Jan Wallin,
Alexandra Wolkowicz, Matthias Baus and the Liverpool Echo and Daily Post.

ISBN 978-1-84631-224-3

The font used throughout this book is called Society, and was designed for the Royal
Liverpool Philharmonic by Liverpool-based design agency, Nonconform.

LIVERPOOL
UNIVERSITY PRESS

The Original Liverpool Sound

The Royal Liverpool Philharmonic Story

Darren Henley & Vincent McKernan

Commissioned photography by Mark McNulty

Supported by CLASSIC *f*M

Acknowledgements

This book would not have been possible without the determination and hard graft of a group of volunteers who worked tirelessly over a two-year period to help to research and catalogue the Royal Liverpool Philharmonic's archive. Each of them deserves enormous thanks for their perseverance and dedication: Doreen Beattie, Hilary Bracey, Sheila Collins, Ralph Crimes, Marjorie Dixon, Lorna Dobson, Eric D. Dunkerley, Phyllis Gibbie, Maureen Graham, Alma Griffiths, Christine Holmes, Alan Jones, Ha-Il Kim, Marion Kilshaw, Anthony Lannigan, Tom Lyon, Maureen Malkinson, Veronica Maguire, Bill McLean, Cecil Pickavance, Joan Pickavance, Christine Roberts, Nancy Rothwell, David Swann, Eira Swann, Elizabeth Smith, Martin Strauss, Tommie Tyndall, John Wallace, Tom Wainwright, Aileen Ward, Jean Whiting and Christine Wright.

Thank you also to the late Vin Tyndall, who was the Honorary Archivist at the Royal Liverpool Philharmonic for more than twenty years. It was his dedication and hard work which ensured the preservation of the Society's unique and irreplaceable archive. The Phil's archive is available for anyone to examine at the Liverpool Record Office and we would like to thank all of the staff at the Record Office, especially David Stoker, the Manager, and Ruth Hobbins, the Senior Archivist, for all of their help and support.

We owe a great debt of thanks to Michael Elliott, the Royal Liverpool Philharmonic's Chief Executive from 2001 to 2008, who asked us to write this book as part of the celebrations of Liverpool's year as European Capital of Culture. Mick's unstinting enthusiasm for the project inspired us to get the job done. Special thanks must go to Andrew Cornall and Jayne Garrity, and also to Sandra Parr, Ian Stephens, Tamsin Cox, Sue Harrison, Michael Eakin, Peter Bounds, Chris Wright, Ian Wright and Geoff Cowie from the Royal Liverpool Philharmonic team for their help; as well as Eric D. Dunkerley, Gordon Reid, John Wallace and Colin Wilkinson for their advice on the text, and to Michael March for designing the book.

The vast majority of this book was written in the Picton Library in the centre of Liverpool. It's a wonderfully inspiring place to write – you should visit it if you have the chance.

Contents

Foreword by Vasily Petrenko

Vasily Petrenko, Principal
Conductor of the Royal Liverpool
Philharmonic Orchestra.

In 1840, a group of music-loving Liverpool businessmen came together to form a society which gave four concerts in its first year. They surely could not have known that, 169 years later, their endeavour would survive and grow as the second-oldest concert promoting society with the oldest continuing professional orchestra in the UK.

Whilst the scope and reach of the Liverpool Phil today is very different, the original vision of that first committee 'to promote the science and practice of music' has remained a constant and driving ambition, and lives and breathes today through the Phil's orchestra, its artists, choirs and staff.

When I was apppointed as Principal Conductor of the Royal Liverpool Philharmonic in 2006, I was only slightly aware of the mantle of tradition which I was to take on. This book is the first time that the illustrious history of the Phil has been fully told. Turning the pages, I hope you will see, as I have come to learn, the true richness and depth of the Phil's history. I am proud to follow in the footsteps of great artists from the 19th and 20th centuries such as Max Bruch, Charles Hallé, Malcolm Sargent, John Pritchard, Charles Groves and Libor Pešek, who have passed on to me the great responsibility of meeting the expectations and ambitions of the Phil's audiences, and of guiding their Orchestra in the 21st century.

Following a year of cultural celebration, in which the Royal Liverpool Philharmonic was the jewel in the City's crown as a central contributor to the 2008 programme of concerts and events, it is very fitting that this book celebrates the achievements of this great cultural institution which has served Liverpool in three centuries.

Vasily Petrenko
Principal Conductor

Introduction

This is the story of the UK's oldest surviving professional symphony orchestra. No other city in the UK can boast a professional orchestra that can trace its continuous history of regular concert-giving, with a formally contracted group of regular players as far back as 1853.

Remarkably, it is the first major hardback book written about the Royal Liverpool Philharmonic in its entire existence. It is also the first book about the Phil to include full-colour photographs. There have been some smaller pamphlets published about the organisation's history over the years; and chapters about the Orchestra have been given over to the Phil in various books about musical life in the City. With the Royal Liverpool Philharmonic Society celebrating its 170th anniversary at the beginning of 2010, we are delighted to be able to right this obvious omission in the history of Liverpool's cultural heritage.

Before we get started, a word about this book. Although we have been fastidious in ensuring that everything that we lay down as fact is historically accurate and supported with extensive documentary evidence, we have tried to tell the story of the Liverpool Phil as a narrative tale. Rather than detailing too many opus numbers and providing extensive musicological examinations of each and every concert performance, we have instead chosen to concentrate on the rich vein of stories about the people and events that bring the Liverpool Phil to life; we have set out to write a book that is for reading and enjoying.

Although this book is an official history, published with the full co-operation of the Royal Liverpool Philharmonic, it has always been important to us as authors that we present an accurate and independent record of the organisation's development. As it unfolds over the next 250 pages, you will come to realise that this is a tale filled with contradictions. Since 1840, the Royal Liverpool Philharmonic has known triumph and disaster, catastrophe and renewal, scandal and propriety, artistic excellence and poor performance, enormous vision and great short-sightedness.

We are lucky to have been the first writers to have access to the Phil's complete archives. After the Royal Liverpool Philharmonic received a grant from the Heritage Lottery Fund, these records were catalogued to an international archival standard. The identifying, sorting and listing took two years to complete and during this process new documents have been uncovered, many of which have never before been written about. We have also been able to reproduce many photographs and illustrations that have never previously been published, alongside others which have not seen the light of day for the best part of a century.

The Royal Liverpool Philharmonic's archive has now moved from the Philharmonic Hall to a new permanent home at the Liverpool Record Office, where it is available for anyone to examine. It is a real treasure chest of musical history, ready for any music lover to explore.

Darren Henley & Vincent McKernan
March 2009

Chapter One

The Musical City

James Clark and Thelma Handy, Joint Leaders,
Royal Liverpool Philharmonic Orchestra.
Photographed at Sefton Park Palm House, Liverpool.

The Booming Port

As the 19th century dawned, Liverpool was second only to London as the most vibrant and economically important place in the whole of England. Britain's international trade had grown furiously towards the end of the 1700s and Liverpool had made best use of its position as one of the country's most accessible ports, both by land and by sea.

The industrial revolution and the need to move goods into and out of the country had made Liverpool a rich city. Throughout the 18th century, Liverpool's docks provided a gateway to the West Indies, North America, Africa and Europe; in the 19th century, India and China were added to this list. It is remarkable to think that in the early 1800s, forty per cent of the entire world's trade was passing through Liverpool.

Raw materials from the heavily industrialised North West of England were exported out of the country via Liverpool and cargoes such as tobacco and cotton were imported back in. The City was also at the centre of the international slave trade, a truth from which Liverpool does not shy away, however unacceptable we find the practice today.

Liverpool's merchants quickly became rich, but the 18th and 19th centuries saw a significant divide between those with burgeoning bank balances and those who had very little at all. The City's population numbers exploded as the workforce grew to meet the demand of the docks and the industries that supported them. People flooded into the area from Ireland, Scotland and Wales and also from mainland Europe. As a result of the trade links with China, a large Chinese community settled in Liverpool, allowing the City to boast the oldest 'China Town' in Europe.

Although the merchant class grew rich, a significant proportion of Liverpool's workers lived in areas of unimaginable filth and deprivation. It was very much a place of 'haves' and 'have-nots'. The City radiated out from the docklands, which were surrounded by an arc of commercial buildings. There was then a sprawling inner-city curve of densely packed housing. The further away from the port that you went, the more pleasant it became. Finally, the poorer quality housing gave way to the far more attractive properties that were the homes of the distinctly better-off townsfolk.

The middle classes enjoyed their growing prosperity and clubs, libraries, concert halls and meeting rooms sprang up in the more fashionable parts of the City. In 1785, work began on building a concert hall on the corner of Bold Street and the appropriately named Concert Street. As many as 1,400 concertgoers were able to enjoy performances given there by up to 150 musicians. When this hall burnt down, a new one was built in its place in 1840. Another music room was opened in Myrtle Street at the same time.

The railways made it far easier to travel long distances across England and the simpler journeys became, the greater the sense of wanderlust of the population at large. Liverpool became the main port for the great shipping companies, such as Cunard and the White Star Line. Many of the most influential thinkers, artists and politicians travelled through Liverpool at one time or another en route to foreign parts.

Musical Beginnings

As the size of Liverpool's middle class grew, so did the appetite for cultural activities. A listing in the *Liverpool Gazette* in 1786 advertises a concert in Ranelagh Gardens on 16th August. It talks of 'music for French horns, clarionets [sic], bassoons, etc, to be followed by Fireworks.' In 1787, the same publication announces concerts in 'the Great Room at George's Coffee House' and also in 'Mr. Wrigley's Great Room.' Eight years later, the *Gazette* advertises performances of *Messiah*, *Jephtha* and *Judas Maccabaeus* conducted by Dr. [Robert] Wainwright. Musical festivals started to become a regular occurrence around the turn of the 19th century, with records of events in 1784, 1790 and 1799.

Around 1820, the Liverpool Music Society was founded. The conductor was Michael Maybrick and its headquarters were in the Old Welsh Schoolroom in Russell Street. The Cecilian Society, a second concert-giving organisation, was formed a little later, with John Jackson as its leader. These two societies seem to have rubbed along rather well, with one concentrating on choral concerts and the other on instrumental performances. Both groups came together to take part in three festivals in 1830, 1833 and 1836.

The star of the 1836 festival was due to be the 29-year-old soprano Maria Malibran, but her untimely death got in the way of her performance. She had been singing in Manchester two weeks before her Liverpool date. Unfortunately, in the middle of Handel's *Messiah*, she had been seized by convulsions. She was carried to the Moseley Arms Hotel, where she died ten days later. Rather than detract from the Liverpool Festival, this event seems to have added to the levels of excitement. The *Liverpool Mail* reported:

The number of fashionable equipages [horse-drawn carriages] in the streets, the gay appearance of the shops, the bustle of the preparations and the groups of strangers to be seen in all directions, forced our attention upon the festivities of the coming week. All the hotels, and hundreds of private houses, are full of visitors, and we believe that at no former period did Liverpool contain so many persons.

Purpose-built venues were thin on the ground, so many of Liverpool's 'musical meetings' took place in churches. The Liverpool Festival Choral Society began its life in 1836, eventually giving its concerts in the Music Hall on Bold Street. At the inaugural concert on 5th March 1839, there was an 'orchestra and chorus complete in every department, consisting of upwards of 100 performers.' As well as summer concerts, the Liverpool Festival Choral Society also presented a performance of *Messiah* each Christmas. In 1841, a list of the members showed 26 sopranos, 15 male altos, 23 tenors and 35 basses.

A Trio of Famous Names

Felix Mendelssohn visited Liverpool in July 1829, after a tour of Scotland. He described the trip in letters back home to his family, with the (as yet incomplete) Liverpool and Manchester Railway among the sights that he took in. His only musical performance was on board an American liner, which was moored at the docks. He ran through what was to become his *Fantasia in F sharp minor, Op. 28* on the ship's Broadwood piano. It turned out that this was the closest he came to giving a concert in Liverpool, although he was to have played a far more pivotal part in Liverpool's musical life, had his death not intervened, as we shall discover later in our story.

Niccolò Paganini visited Liverpool twice during his tours of England and Scotland. This series of performances around the country made him a wealthy man. In 1832, he gave four concerts at Liverpool's Theatre Royal and two years later made two appearances at the Royal Amphitheatre. During his first trip, he performed his *Violin Concerto No. 3* for the first time.

The Liverpool-based Rockliff and Duckworth published a *Memoir of Paganini* in 1832. It goes into great detail about one particular performance by Paganini in Liverpool:

His fame had of course preceded him; and though the price of admission was greater than at any other place out of London, his concerts were attended by all the beauty and fashion, not only of the town, but of the neighbourhood. Williamson Square was nightly crowded with equipages; and all who went to hear him returned enraptured.

15

Above. Felix Mendelssohn.

Above right. Niccolò Paganini.

Right. Franz Liszt.

16

Nobody was more enraptured than the anonymous writer, who went on to describe the moment that Paganini came on stage:

> He enters the orchestra, bending and smiling (but what a ghastly smile!) – a sallow, haggard, ungraceful spectre – and with his instrument clutched rather than held in his lean, clawlike fingers – you would as soon expect melody from a sepulchre. A few seconds elapse, the burst of applause subsides, and a change comes over the musician … his figure grows erect, his attitude commanding, his features stern and thoughtful: he is brooding over the mystery and you expect, with breathless eagerness, its disclosure … The orchestra now, upon repetition of his wild gesture, begin a striking movement, and at once, from the concluding crash of the instruments, starts out Paganini's long, glistening tone, the beginning of a strain of delicious melody, chaste yet passionate in expression … and of a clear far-reaching power which searches your heart's centre.

The third of our trio of big names who visited Liverpool around this time was Franz Liszt – another dramatic performer on the platform. In 1840, he was 29 years old and was at the height of his fame. His existence was more akin to the pop stars of today than how we tend to think of life as a classical musician.

One of the other musicians who toured with Liszt, a Welshman called John Orlando Parry, describes their visit to Liverpool in his diary:

> Dec. 1st. Left Chester at 11 – arrived Birkenhead at $\frac{1}{4}$ to 1 – had Oysters Pickled, Bread and Cheese in the open air at the Hotel garden!! We enjoyed it very much – Liszt treated us all – Boat arrived – crossed to Liverpool – Liszt all alive on board – put on his Hungarian great bear skin cloak – Everyone thinking he was a little touched … dressed and went to the Theatre Royal were [sic] the concert was held … the house was so full many left directly Liszt had played his last piece.

> Dec. 2nd. Walked about Liverpool – bought some spectacles for Liszt – at 2 $\frac{1}{2}$ we went to railway.

Liszt and his musicians travelled to Preston, Rochdale and Manchester before coming back to Liverpool. After a weekend's relaxation, they journeyed on to Dublin.

1840 was not just an auspicious year in the history of music in Liverpool because of Liszt's visit; it was also the year that saw the birth of the Liverpool Philharmonic Society. Although its founding fathers had been meeting regularly to practise and perform choral music for some years, the Society formally came into being on 10th January 1840. Liverpool's musical life was never to look back.

Chapter Two

The Early Days

Jonathan Small. Principal Oboe, Royal Liverpool
Philharmonic Orchestra. Photographed at Liverpool Marina.

THE FIRST
QUARTERLY PERFORMANCE
OF THE
LIVERPOOL PHILHARMONIC SOCIETY,

WILL TAKE PLACE AT

MR. LASSELL'S SALOON, GREAT RICHMOND-STREET,

On THURSDAY, the 12th of MARCH, 1840.

Conductor............ Mr. JOHN RUSSELL.

Leader............ Mr. H. F. ALDRIDGE, Jun.

Organist............ Mr. WM. SUDLOW.

PROGRAMME.

PART I.

OVERTURE .... (First time in Liverpool.) .... Kalliwoda.

GLEE .... " Chough and Crow." .... Bishop.
Solo parts by Miss HAMMOND, Miss ALDRIDGE and Mr. WEARING.

MADRIGAL .... " Fire ! Fire !" .... Thomas Morley, 1594.

ROUND .... " The Sun has been long on Old Mont Blanc." .... Bishop.
Miss HAMMOND, Miss ALDRIDGE and Miss M. SWAIN.

" MUSIC IN MACBETH." .... M. Locke.
Solo parts, Misses SWAIN and HAMMOND, and Messrs. DODD and SUTTON.

FINALE CHORUS .... " Bright Orb." .... Bishop.
Solo parts, Miss HAMMOND, Miss M. SWAIN and Mr. DODD.

PART II.

OVERTURE .... " La Fiancée." ......(First time in Liverpool) .... Auber.

CHORUS .... " Fair as a Bride."......(William Tell) .... Rossini.

MADRIGAL .... " Flora gave me." .... Wilbye, 1598.

SESTETTO .... Piano Forte, Flute, Clarionet, Horn, Violoncello, and Contra-Basso...... Onslow.
Messrs. ALDRIDGE, jun. FISHER, LEONARD, THOMPSON, TIVENDELL and TAYLEURE.

TRIO, from Azor and Zemira .... " Night's ling'ring shades." .... Spohr.
Miss SWAIN, Miss ALDRIDGE and Miss M. SWAIN.

GLEE .... " Where art thou, Beam of Light." .... Bishop.
The Misses SWAIN and Messrs. DODD and WEARING.

FINALE CHORUS .... " Loud let the Moorish tambours sound." .... Bishop.
Solo parts, The Misses SWAIN.

Doors will be opened at Seven o'Clock, and the Concert commence at Half-past Seven precisely.

The Committee respectfully request, that, as the Concert will terminate at an early hour, the Company will
await the conclusion of the Performance.

Carriages to set down and take up, with the Horses' heads towards St. Ann's Church.

The Society is Born

The men behind the launch of the Liverpool Philharmonic Society may well have had great aspirations for the organisation from its earliest days, but they started out by running relatively small concerts at a 'saloon' at the back of a dance academy on Great Richmond Street run by a Mr Lassell.

This is what was performed at the very first concert on 12th March 1840:

Overture	Kalliwoda
Glee 'The Chough and the Crow'	Bishop
Madrigal 'Fire, fire my heart'	Thomas Morley
Round 'The Sun has been long on Mont Blanc'	Bishop
The Music in 'Macbeth'	Matthew Locke
Final Chorus 'Bright Orb'	Bishop

Overture 'La Fiancée' [First time in Liverpool]	Auber
Chorus 'Fair as a Bride' (from William Tell)	Rossini
Madrigal 'Flora gave me fairest flowers'	Wylbye
Sestetto (Flute, Clarinet, Horn, Cello, Contra Bass, Pianoforte)	George Onslow
Trio 'Night's ling'ring Shade' (from 'Azor and Zemira')	Spohr
Glee 'Where art thou, beam of light?'	Bishop
Final Chorus 'Loud let the Moorish tambours sound'	Bishop

Conductor: John Russell
Leader: H.F. Aldridge, Jnr.
Organist: William Sudlow

RULES

OF THE

LIVERPOOL PHILHARMONIC SOCIETY.

ESTABLISHED 10TH JANUARY, 1840.

I.—The Society to be conducted and managed by a Committee, the number not to exceed thirty six; five to form a quorum, the Treasurer, Secretary, Conductor, and Organist, being Members of such Committee, *ex officio. The Treasurer and Secretary to be appointed at the General Annual Meeting.*

II.—The Rehearsals to be held on such Monday evenings as shall be appointed by the Committee.

III.—There shall be Twelve Concerts in the year, viz:—Four Quarterly Full Dress Concerts, with metropolitan talent, and Eight Monthly Undress Concerts, with local talent.

IV.—The subscriptions to be as follow:—*Reserved Gallery.*—For Two Tickets, transferable to Ladies and Strangers and members of the family, with privilege of introducing a Lady or Stranger to the Eight Monthly Concerts, £2; Extra Single Annual Tickets, issued to subscribers of £2 for members of the family, *not* transferable, 15s; Single Tickets, transferable as above, with privilege of introducing a Lady or Stranger to the Eight Monthly Concerts, £1 5s.—*Body of the Room.*—For Three Tickets, transferable to Ladies and Strangers and members of the family, with the same privilege as subscribers to the Reserved Gallery, £2; for Two Tickets, ditto ditto, £1 10s; Extra Single Annual Tickets, issued to subscribers of £2 or £1 10s, for members of the family, *not* transferable, 10s; Single Tickets, transferable as above, with privilege of introducing a Lady or Stranger to the Eight Monthly Concerts, £1. The Upper Gallery will be reserved for the use of the Pupils of the Liverpool Collegiate Institution; the Annual Subscription for a Non-transferable Ticket, 5s; Practical Performing Members, for Two Tickets for the Body of the Room, with the like privilege and restrictions, 10s 6d; ditto ditto, for Two Tickets to the Reserved Gallery, £1 1s.

V.—The Committee shall have the power of admitting Members, duly proposed and seconded, in writing, and their names (so admitted) shall be registered into an "Admission" Book, to be provided for that purpose.

VI.—The Entrance Money to be 10s 6d, in order to form a Fund for the purchase of the Organ, now lent on hire, and for the liquidation of other extraordinary expenses.

VII.—The Committee to have the power to avail themselves of the services of any professional lady or gentleman who may be required to complete the orchestra; and such lady or gentleman shall, in consideration of

Although John Russell conducted this first concert, he shared the job with Thomas Clough and with William Sudlow, who was also made Secretary of the Society, a role that would be equivalent to being Chief Executive today.

There is no doubt that the leading lights in the Society took their roles very seriously, with an onerous set of no fewer than seventeen rules being laid out, which covered everything from who had responsibility for choosing the repertoire at the concerts through to a detailed system of fines for non-attendance at rehearsals. By 1843, a set of additional 'Laws for the Regulation of the Orchestra' were also published.

Things were going well. So well, in fact, that the Society needed more space for its concerts. Leaving 'Mr. Lassell's Saloon' behind, the Society began giving performances in the hall of the Collegiate Institute, in Shaw Street.

Unquestionably, the Liverpool Philharmonic of the mid and late 19th century existed purely for the pleasure of the moneyed merchant class in the town, in stark contrast to the Royal Liverpool Philharmonic of today. The concerts given in this period were sometimes of the 'grand full dress' and sometimes of the 'undress' order. One concert, on 27th April 1843, is described as being one of the 'grand toilet affairs.'

In the same year, J. Zeugheer Herrmann was appointed the Liverpool Philharmonic Society's Principal Conductor, a job he was to keep through until his death in 1865.

J. Zeugheer Herrmann

Born: Zurich, 1805
Died: 1865
Principal Conductor: 1843-1865

Born Jakob Zeugheer, he had changed his name to J. Zeugheer Herrmann by the time he arrived in Liverpool in 1843. A well respected violin player, he had toured with his own string quartet and had spent time in England, Scotland and Ireland. Between 1831 and 1838, he was the conductor of the Manchester Gentlemen's Concerts. Away from the concert platform, he composed a range of different instrumental music, as well as an opera and a series of choral works. He did much to develop the Liverpool Philharmonic as a professional orchestra, although his relationship with the Society – and the choir in particular – was at times particularly fractious.

On 23rd May 1844, the Liverpool Philharmonic Society's orchestra performed its first symphonies in a concert: Haydn's *Symphony No. 99 in E flat* and Beethoven's *Symphony No. 1 in C major*. Repeatedly around this time, concertgoers were begged either to leave the hall during the interval or to stay until the end of the final piece and not simply to get up and leave in the middle of a performance.

1844 was a significant year in the Society's development. Alongside the arrival of the symphony and the new Principal Conductor making his presence felt, the Liverpool-based architect John Cunningham was asked to prepare plans for a hall which would be situated on Hope Street at the junction with Myrtle Street.

The initial prospectus estimated that '£4,000 at the least will be required to meet the purchase of the Land and for the erection of the Building, which sum it is proposed shall be raised by issuing 400 shares of £10 each.' These shares were payable in four instalments. This initial prospectus talked of a 'Concert Room, capable of holding 1,500 persons.' However, by the 2nd September 1844, the Society issued a new prospectus. Gone was the plan for a 'Concert Room' and in its place was a far grander 'New Concert Hall':

> The Hall is intended to contain in the Audience part, two thousand one
> hundred persons, and on the Orchestra two hundred and fifty, and to embrace
> every requisite convenience in the shape of refreshment and retiring rooms.

The cost of a single share, bringing with it one concert ticket, was twelve guineas; a double share (two tickets) was eighteen guineas and a treble share (three tickets) was twenty-four guineas. With a further subscription charge payable to the Society each year, the financial burdens of being a member were pretty steep.

The prospectus also dangles in front of the Society's richest members a way of propelling themselves into a new social cachet by buying seats in one of the boxes to be built along the sides of the new hall:

> To meet the repeatedly expressed wishes of many members of the
> Society, it is proposed to appropriate a proportion of the side galleries of
> the new Hall in the following manner:-

By dividing the first and second row of seats on each side into twenty compartments, each to contain six persons, three on each row, to be styled Proprietary Boxes, and to be appropriated in perpetuity to such members as shall, instead of taking their allotted shares as already detailed, subscribe and pay down a sum, varying from One Hundred and Ten to Eighty Guineas, according to situation, for each box, with an annual subscription equalling in amount three double subscriptions at the rate fixed by the General Committee.

The fund-raising was a slow process and, in the meantime, concerts continued in the Collegiate Hall. In 1845, there was an even greater sense of permanence to the Society, with a list of the band being given on a concert programme for the first time. A newly published set of rules stipulates that there will be four 'full-dress concerts with metropolitan talent' and six 'undress concerts' each year. The 'metropolitan talent' engaged during this period includes W. Sterndale Bennett, Alboni, Grisi, Mario, Tamburini and Joachim – all major box office draws in their day.

The Society's rules were rather draconian and seem to have been designed largely to keep as many people as possible out of the concert hall. They state that 'no gentleman within 7 miles of Liverpool, not being a member, or a member in the family of a member, shall be admitted to any concert' and that 'if any subscriber interrupt the performance or become troublesome to the Society' he might be black-balled. The subscription rates for the concerts operated on a sliding scale. In the reserved gallery and the main body of Collegiate Hall, one seat cost £1 11s 6d and a pair of seats £2 12s 6d. For three seats, the charge was £3 18s 6d, with any further seats being sold at a flat rate of £1. In the upper gallery, one seat set a concertgoer back £1, two seats £1 10s and three seats £2, with the price of additional seats set at 10s.

In 1846, the foundation stone was laid for the new hall and the proper building work started the following year. On 20th December 1847, the Society noted that:

The committee of the Liverpool Philharmonic Society had arranged with Dr Mendelssohn to superintend the opening of their new concert hall, for which occasion he was about to write a cantata. The words selected for this work were from Milton's *Comus*.

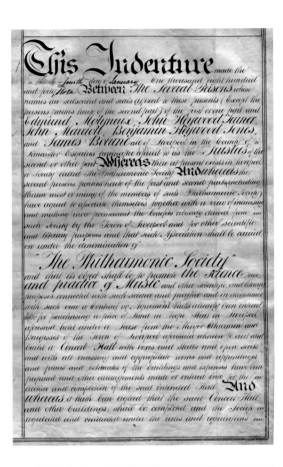

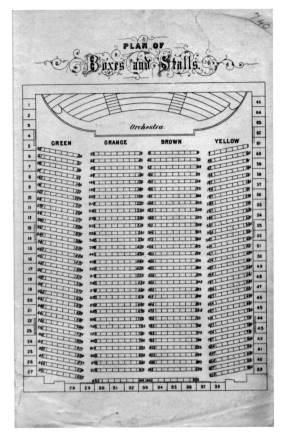

The original Deed of the Liverpool Philharmonic Society 1847. The stated object of the Society was 'to promote the science and practice of Music'.

Plan of boxes and stalls, original Philharmonic Hall.

The programme for the First Full Dress Concert of the season in 1843 at the Collegiate Hall.

The prospectus for the building of Philharmonic Hall.

Minute authorising the payment of
£105 to Mendelssohn for composing
a work for the new Hall.

Advertisement for the opening of
Philharmonic Hall in 1849.

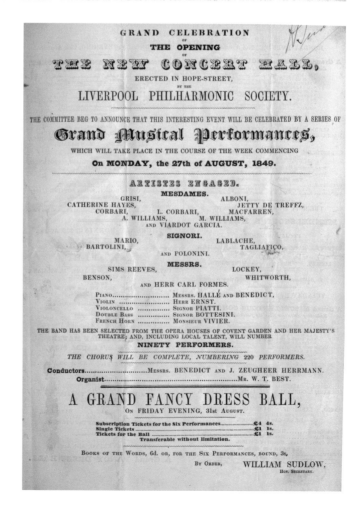

This was a sign of the Society's enormous ambition. To have secured the services of Felix Mendelssohn, possibly the world's most highly regarded living composer at the time, shows the determination of the committee to put Liverpool on the musical map.

Unfortunately, Mendelssohn was not to be a living composer for much longer and the Society was plunged into gloom on the announcement of his untimely death. Any plans he may have had for *Comus* died with him, without a note being written down. This setback appears to have had very little effect on the scale of the plans for the hall's grand opening.

A Home of its Own

In the end, it cost £30,000 to build the hall. *The Times* noted that although this was 'a high figure, [it] was nothing extraordinary for such a rich commercial town as Liverpool'. By the time the hall opened, there were already seven hundred subscribers who had purchased either a box or a stalls seat in perpetuity, so long as they continued to pay their annual subscription to the Society. Between them, these seven hundred individuals owned all sixty-five of the boxes and more than six hundred of the sixteen hundred stalls seats.

At this stage, there was absolutely no question of the hall being used for anything other than concerts promoted by the Society. *The Times* reported:

> The subject has been mooted of opening the hall, when not required for
> the concerts, for other than musical purposes; but this has been
> strenuously opposed in many quarters, and cannot be decided upon
> except at a general meeting of the entire body of proprietors.

The New Concert Hall opened with much fanfare on Monday, 27th August 1849. The evening included performances from three of the Liverpool Philharmonic's future Principal Conductors: Alfred Mellon (who played in the violins), Julius Benedict (who shared the conducting duties with Zeugheer Herrmann, as well as performing a piano solo) and Charles Hallé (who was also a piano soloist).

The opening week included 'grand miscellaneous' concerts on the Monday, Tuesday and Wednesday evenings; Mendelssohn's *Elijah* on the Tuesday morning; Handel's *Messiah* on the Thursday morning and Rossini's *Stabat Mater* and Mendelssohn's *Lauda Sion* on the Friday morning. The Friday night was taken up by a 'Grand Fancy Dress Ball.'

The choral concerts included an ambitious 320 performers, with 96 players in the orchestra. The choir consisted of 64 sopranos, 39 altos, 56 tenors and 55 basses.

The Times reported the opening festivities in detail, with far more space being given to events in Liverpool than would ever appear in a national newspaper these days. This was not just a major event in Liverpool; it was big news on a national stage:

> The interest attached to this grand musical meeting appears to be immense. The town is full of bustle; arrivals from all parts of the country are incessant, and the hotels will doubtless reap a rich harvest.

The un-named critic was particularly impressed with the new concert hall, describing it as:

> … one of the finest and best adapted to music that I ever entered. The method of lighting is quite novel: there are no chandeliers or lustres either in the centre of the ceiling or on the sides of the room, but one unbroken line of small gas lights along the top of the cornice over the arches, which gives the appearance of a single belt of light all round the hall … The hall was filled with ladies attired in the most elegant full dress, which the new manner of lighting displayed with unaccustomed brilliancy.

The Times noted that with the as yet unfinished St. George's Hall, Liverpool was lucky enough to have two major concert halls, while London 'cannot boast one grand music room.'

Interior of Philharmonic Hall, c.1930.

Watercolour of the interior of Philharmonic Hall, 1854.

Plan showing the route taken by carriages at Philharmonic Hall, 1851.

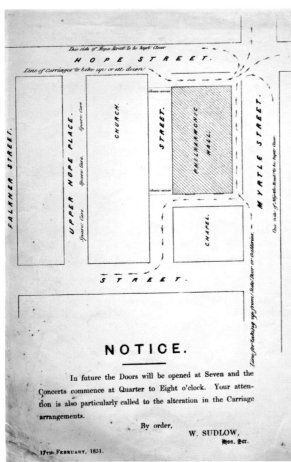

The hall was not full on the opening night. *The Times* correspondent is clear about where the blame lay for this:

> … the very high price of admission – one guinea to any part of the hall not occupied by the subscribers – must have kept and will again keep, numbers of the general public away.

There was another reason that many potential concertgoers stayed away. An anonymous letter published by one of the local newspapers claimed that the building was unsafe because it had no central support pillars. It was suggested that the roof could cave in on the unsuspecting audience below.

The news that those who attended the opening night survived the concert without being crushed must have spread, because *The Times* reports a bigger crowd for the performance of *Elijah:*

> The hall was better filled than last night; but we are disposed to think that unless the Committee offer greater facility to the general public there will not be one really crowded attendance during the festival.

The correspondent returns to his theme the following day, with a surprisingly trenchant attack on the Society's elitism:

> The Liverpool public complain bitterly of the exclusive system adopted by the Committee of the Society, who have placed the charges of admission to non-subscribers at so high a figure as one guinea. Without entering at present in to the merits of the dispute, we must confess that this looks like a determination to restrain the middle and humbler classes from enjoying the greatest musical treat which the festival offers. The population of Liverpool may be divided into three sections – the rich, the middling rich, and the poor. In the present case the rich have it all to themselves, the festival being confined to the proprietors of the Philharmonic Concert Hall, the subscribers, and the press, since a guinea in these times for a musical entertainment, no matter how attractive, is out of the power of any but the affluent to give. The local press also appear to have been grumbling about the scanty

accommodation afforded them, and from these two sources united has sprung up a feeling of hostility against the Society, in which originated the stupid report of the building being unsafe, and the other insinuations inimical to the well doing of the festival. It is certain that had the spacious galleries been thrown open to the public at a reasonable price – say 10s 6d stalls, and 5s back seats – the hall would have been crammed at both morning and evening performances; the Committee would have added a large sum to their fund, and the interest among all classes, in favour of the Society and its professed object of elevating the taste for the art in Liverpool, would have been warm and unanimous. As it is, we think, the glorious opportunity has been thrown away, or, at least, trifled with, of distinguishing this great commercial place among the musical towns of Europe.

Those who could afford to pay the entry price would probably have gone home feeling that they had been given value for money because the concerts were anything but short, another fact noted by the man from *The Times* after Wednesday evening's 'Grand Miscellaneous Concert':

> Another concert of four hours and a quarter in duration! When will the directors of music festivals take into consideration the wholesome adage 'Enough is as good as a feast?'

The hall was seen as a design triumph and resulted in a good deal of praise for its architect, John Cunningham. When he died in 1873, his obituary in *The Builder* noted:

> The building which obtained for him the most reputation is the Philharmonic Hall ... the music-room in which, 135 ft. by 100 ft., was for some time the largest there [in Liverpool], and has received high praise from musicians. We are not prepared to record it as a perfect concert-room. It is remarkably free from echo; but, on the other hand, it is not a resonant room, owing to the extensive use of plaster, and the great amount of upholstery, which rather damps the sound than assists it. It was undoubtedly the best room of the time it was built.

Herrmann's Manifesto for the New Orchestra

By the end of 1849, Zeugheer Herrmann felt confident enough in his own position to write to the Chairman and the Committee, outlining his thoughts on how the Society's orchestra should be run:

> I should like, sir, to impress your Committee strongly with my conviction that the perfect success of the Society can never depend on the artists which you may bring down from London, which of course must greatly vary in interest and capabilities, there being but very few names who command success, and those cannot often be secured. Our real strength must lie in our own forces, it must become acknowledged that the Society possesses an excellent band, an excellent Chorus, and that everything that depends on them is sure to be well done. We must work for the honour of gaining a distinguished place among the musical establishments of England.

Herrmann's letter runs to ten handwritten pages. He goes on to discuss the orchestra's make-up:

> As we could not expect with the means at our command to be able to form a large band, I should recommend at present to engage by the year and with honourable salaries a small but select band, obliging its members to meet weekly, and expecting their services for any unlimited number of concerts which your committee may feel disposed to give during the year; the remainder might be engaged by the Concert with one or two rehearsals, and with a palpable difference in their remuneration.

In two appendices at the end of the letter, Herrmann sets out exactly how he would like these two orchestras to look:

Appendix No. 1. Construction of the small [sic] regular Philharmonic Band:

First Violins	One principal and 4 others
Second detto	One principal and 4 others
Tenors	One principal and 2 others
Violoncelli	One principal and 2 others
Bassi	Detto
2 Flutes	
2 Clarinetts	
2 Oboi	
2 Fagotti	
2 Corni	
2 Trumpets and Tympani	

Total 32.

Appendix No. 2. Grand Band

At least 12 first Violins with principal

At least 12 second Violins with principal

At least 8 Tenors with principal

At least 6 Violoncelli with principal

At least 6 Contrabassi with principal

2 Flutes

2 Obois

2 Bassoons

2 Clarinetts

4 Corni

2 Trumpetts

3 Trombonis

1 Tympani

Total 63.

Chorus of Discontent

By 1850, the members of the choir created their own organisation, the Liverpool Philharmonic Auxiliary Society. They waged a long-term battle with Zeugheer Herrmann, which reached crisis point in 1850, following a performance of Mendelssohn's *Elijah*. The spat centred on the speed at which Herrmann took the work. The members of the choir vowed to teach their conductor a lesson by taking things at their own pace, but the orchestra followed Herrmann's beat and, in the end, the choir fell into line.

The choir called a meeting and passed a resolution blaming Herrmann for the debacle. The conductor was outraged and immediately fired off an angry letter. He was persuaded to withdraw it and instead wrote a second letter, which was handed over to the members of the Auxiliary Society's committee.

They passed a second resolution, the details of which are outlined by the main Society's secretary, William Sudlow, in a letter to his Committee on 23rd March 1850. He does not pull any punches:

> They consider the letter [from Herrmann] most offensive, imparting as he does, all the blame to them and unjustly attempting to throw odium on the whole Body [the choir] …

> They consider, although fully admitting it to be the duty of band and Chorus to follow the Conductor's time, right or wrong, that, in the present case it was not possible – and no Body of Choristers and Band can steadily follow an irregular Beat …

> They consider that a Conductor should not rehearse at one time and beat in another at the performance, which was the case in the present instance.

Sudlow suggests to the Committee that the members of the choir are not being given the attention they deserve and recommends that the members of the main Committee take a greater interest in their output. Herrmann's tendency to fire off angry missives has also tried Sudlow's patience and he finishes the letter by saying:

I may with confidence express my belief, that the slightest concession on the part of Mr Herrmann, would be satisfactory and restore harmony and good feeling and if Mr Herrmann would (as I am sorry to say he has not hitherto done) only reciprocate the forbearance and good temper which have ever displayed towards himself, by the Body [the choir], I can safely say the most satisfactory results might be anticipated.

Herrmann did not take the hint and tendered his resignation two days later. His letter was far shorter than many that he wrote to the Committee, but it has more than a touch of melodrama about it:

To the Chairman and Gentlemen of the Committee of the Liverpool Philharmonic Socty.

Sir, and Gentlemen

After your resolution of to-day it cannot surprise you to receive my resignation of the honourable post I have held for some years in your Society.

I had hoped that my labours and the acknowledged results from them would have secured me from the receipt of such a resolution, even if, for once, I had committed a fault of some magnitude, which however my conscience still acquits me of on the last occasion.

This being probably my last communication with you, I take this opportunity of thanking you sincerely for the many proofs of kindness which I have received from your committee during my connexion with the Society.

I am

Sir and Gentlemen,

Your Obedt. Sevt.

J. Zeugheer Herrmann

25th of March 1850

36 Bedford St. South

Herrmann's resignation was not accepted and he remained as the Liverpool Philharmonic's Principal Conductor until his death. His fractious relationship with the choir was patched over. The main Committee pointed out that the orchestra was 'unequalled in the Town as a permanent establishment' and that the chorus was 'admitted by the best judges to be inferior to none in the Kingdom.' The choir remained a rebellious bunch, even going on strike at one stage. They also complained about the 'arbitrary and capricious temper' of their chorus master, William Sudlow, although, considering that he was also the Society's Secretary and Treasurer, it is unsurprising that their murmurings of discontent went largely unheeded. Despite all of the moaning from the singers, the choir continued to grow and by December 1851, when it performed Handel's *Messiah*, it was 180 strong.

Money Troubles

In January 1852 a committee was appointed to 'investigate the affairs of the Philharmonic Society with a view to devise measures for extricating it from its present embarrassments' – in other words, money was tight. The building of the new concert hall had left the Society with a deficit and a mortgage. The committee recommended a new five-year plan to return the Society to the black. Reference is made in this report to the size of the Philharmonic Society's 'band, consisting of fifty three performers.' It is important to note that this was a full five years before Charles Hallé formed the Manchester-based orchestra, which took his name – but more of that, later in our story.

The committee's report examined a number of different options for improving the Society's parlous financial situation. The committee noted that 'the Society possesses what sooner or later will become a valuable property in the 183 seats still unappropriated, and they advise that none of these should be disposed of under the original price of Eighteen Guineas.'

The possibility of relaxing the rules for admission to the Society's concerts was also mooted:

> It has been discussed also whether the restriction to the admission of Resident Non-Subscribers might not be repealed, without loss to the Society, and to the

convenience, and probably to the pecuniary advantage, of the Shareholders. The Committee, however, are divided upon the point, and they leave it to the decision of the Meeting.

The meeting of the Proprietors came down firmly against the idea, passing the Resolution that 'the restrictive clause with regard to Resident Gentlemen be retained.' The Committee also recommended retaining high seat prices:

> A large reduction in the price of admission into the Gallery was also hinted at, but this the Committee think would not be remunerative, and would be undesirable in other aspects.

The optimism of the first decade of the Society's existence seemed to be fading under the shadow of financial gloom, with the Committee's report finishing ominously:

> The embarrassed state of the Society creates doubt and distrust, and paralyzes the exertions of all concerned with it. A single bad season, whether rising from commercial distress, or from any of those causes which periodically affect the prosperity of all communities, would plunge the Society deeper into debt, till Liverpool may have the mortification to witness the sad spectacle of one of her Institutions, established for the cultivation of an elegant and refined science, and combining amongst its Members a great portion of the wealth, intelligence and respectability of the town, languishing for a few years in extreme poverty, and then expiring, under an accumulated load of debt, in the arms of a sheriff's officer.

As a background to these financial woes, keeping the high-maintenance Principal Conductor happy appears to have been a major preoccupation of the Society's ruling Committee. In a letter written on 9th February 1853, Zeugheer Herrmann makes his feelings more than clear:

> I am put at the head of a band containing many fine performers and musicians, but also some utterly unfit for the place in a concert like those of your Society ... Very frequently, indeed mostly, I get my first intimation of who is to sing or play at the concerts from the placards on the wall ... I have had offered frequently and at the last hour Piano Forte parts to

conduct from which did not correspond with the orchestral parts at all …
I have felt like a stranger amongst you, enjoying politeness when in
personal intercourse but not cordiality.

A week later, in another letter, he returns to his theme:

I request you will let me have, as early as possible, a Copy of your
Programmes, and that I might be entitled to suggest alterations … May I
request a List of the Band now engaged for the coming Season, that I may
know on what I have to depend.

In October 1853, the Committee responded to a complaint about a Member who
admitted unauthorised persons into his stall:

Sir, the Committee having been informed that you were present at the
Subscription Concert on the 4th Inst. think it possible you are not aware
that Residents (not being Proprietors or Subscribers) are not admissible to
these Concerts. They feel it right to give you this information, being sure
that you have no desire to transgress the Rules of the Society.

In the same year, an extra concert was given for the benefit of William Sudlow, 'in
testimony of his invaluable services as honorary secretary of the Liverpool
Philharmonic Society and conductor of the vocal rehearsals'.

Rocked by Scandal

William Sudlow had played an important part in setting up the Society, acting as the
Honorary Secretary, the Vocal Conductor and one of the Society's first orchestral
conductors. He had worked tirelessly for the benefit of the Society – or at least that
was how it had appeared up until the moment when it was discovered that fiddling at
the Phil had not been confined to the ranks of the violins.

On 13th January 1855, William Sudlow wrote to the Committee tendering his
resignation. Although his behaviour had clearly been dishonourable, the tone of the
letter makes no excuses for what he had done:

> I do not attempt, in any way, to justify my conduct … I do not claim the
> slightest credit for any services I have rendered the Society … I
> therefore humbly and confidently hope, that my painful position,
> although unjustifiable, will meet with considerate deliberation … It will
> be to the last moment of my life, my never ceasing regret and reproach,
> that my connection with a Society, which has had my best exertions and
> entire devotion, should be severed in such an unfortunate manner.

The Committee employed professional accountants to examine the books and
discovered that Sudlow's 'defalcations' had robbed the Society of £2,424 14s. In
today's money, this would be the equivalent of around £150,000. As a member of
the Society, no direct action was taken against Sudlow, other than to accept his
resignation. However, the Committee's report into the matter was damning:

> The Committee would have hailed with satisfaction any circumstances which
> might have been pleaded in palliation of his grave offence; but they confess
> with deep concern their inability to discover a single extenuating fact. The
> examination of the accounts, on the contrary, has disclosed an artful and
> systematic course of fraud and deception, commencing as far back as the
> beginning of 1853, and continued up to the moment of his detection.

The investigation showed that Sudlow diverted funds to himself without entering
them into the cash book, as well as withholding cheques to other people who were
entitled to them. Although there were regular audits of the accounts, Sudlow was
always around to proffer an explanation or to divert attention away from his
misdemeanours. His position had allowed him to gain the trust of the other members
of the Society and no detailed questions had been asked for a number of years.

The effect on the fledgling Society's finances could easily have been disastrous, but
the Committee chairman, Hardman Earle, was relieved to report that 'the only
pecuniary effect of this vexatious event will be to postpone for two or three years the
final liquidation of the debt, through the growing prosperity of the Society'.

An advertisement was placed for a paid Secretary. Out of the 63 applicants,
somewhat surprisingly, it was a distant relative of the disgraced William Sudlow who

was given the job. Henry Sudlow was cut from different cloth though, serving the Society for three decades without the slightest whiff of impropriety.

Away from the behind-the-scenes machinations, the Society was bringing some famous names to Liverpool. The Society relented on its policy of only allowing musical events in the Philharmonic Hall. In 1852, Charles Dickens brought his theatrical company, the Guild of Literature & Art, to perform in the Hall. He and Wilkie Collins acted in three plays. The same year saw an appearance at the Hall by William Makepeace Thackeray. In 1856, there were performances from the 'Swedish nightingale', Jenny Lind, from the pianist (and husband of Robert), Clara Schumann, and from Charles Hallé. In 1858, Charles Dickens returned to give a series of readings and his signature appears in the Society's Vistors' Book. 1858 was a significant year for the Society all around, with the mortgage on the Hall also being paid off.

Money Matters

Just as they do today, the big names in classical music demanded big payments. In 1861, Adelina Patti was paid £400 for two concerts. Three years later, she received £500 for two concert appearances. It was a sign of just how good a shape the Society's finances were in that these payments could be made. By now, a reserve fund was even set aside, just in case the state of the Society's finances ever became parlous once again.

In 1862, the Society hosted the world première performance of Rossini's *Bolero,* a duet performed by the Marchisio sisters. Later that year, there was a performance from 28-year-old Charles Santley, well on the way to becoming the most popular English baritone of Victorian and Edwardian times. Santley was one of Liverpool's own and there was consternation from some members of the Society at the fee he was charging.

Santley's father was a Liverpool-based bookbinder, organist and music teacher. Alongside his father and sister, Kate, the young Charles had sung in the Liverpool Philharmonic Society chorus only a few years previously. But, after learning his craft in Italy, his star had risen far above that of a chorus member. He was to

Philharmonic Hall, Liverpool.

Manager, Mr. CHARLES DICKENS, Tavistock House, Tavistock Square, in the County of Middlesex.

On FRIDAY EVENING, SEPTEMBER 3rd, 1852,
THE AMATEUR COMPANY
OF THE

GUILD OF LITERATURE & ART;

To encourage Life Assurance and other Provident Habits among Authors and Artists; to render such assistance to both as shall never compromise their independence; and to found a new Institution where honourable rest from arduous labour shall still be associated with the discharge of congenial duties;

WILL HAVE THE HONOR OF PRESENTING
(THIS BEING THEIR LAST NIGHT OF PERFORMANCE,)
THE PETITE COMEDY, IN TWO ACTS, OF

USED UP.

SIR CHARLES COLDSTREAM, BART.,		Mr. CHARLES DICKENS,
SIR ADONIS LEECH,		Mr. COE,
THE HONORABLE TOM SAVILLE,		Mr. JOHN TENNIEL,
WURZEL, (a Farmer)		Mr. F. W. TOPHAM,
JOHN IRONBRACE, (a Blacksmith)		Mr. MARK LEMON,
MR. FENNEL, (a Lawyer)		Mr. AUGUSTUS EGG, A.R.A.
JAMES,		Mr. WILKIE COLLINS,
MARY,		Mrs. HENRY COMPTON,
LADY CLUTTERBUCK,		Mrs. COE.

SCENERY.

Saloon in Sir Charles Coldstream's House,	Painted by Mr. PITT,
Distant View of the River,	" Mr. STANFIELD, R.A.
Interior of an Old Farm House,	" Mr. PITT.

Previous to the Play the Band will Perform an OVERTURE, composed expressly for this purpose, by Mr. C. COOTE, (Pianist to his His Grace the Duke of Devonshire);
WHO WILL, ON THIS OCCASION, PRESIDE AT THE PIANOFORTE.

After which, the Historical Drama, in Two Acts, by J. R. PLANCHE, Esq., called

CHARLES XII.

CHARLES THE TWELFTH, (King of Sweden)		Mr. FRANK STONE, A.R.A.
GENERAL DUCKERT, (Governor of Stralsund)		Mr. COE,
COLONEL REICHEL,		Mr. PETER CUNNINGHAM,
GUSTAVUS DE MERVELT,		Mr. JOHN TENNIEL,
MAJOR VANBERG, (under the assumed name of FIRMANN)		Mr. AUGUSTUS EGG, A.R.A.
ADAM BROCK, (a Wealthy Farmer)		Mr. F. W. TOPHAM.
TRIPTOLEMUS MUDDLEWORTH, (Burgomaster)		Mr. WILKIE COLLINS.
ULRICA, (Daughter of Vanberg)		Miss FANNY YOUNG.
EUDIGA, (Daughter of Adam Brock)		Mrs. HENRY COMPTON.

SCENERY.

Public Ground and Inn,	Mr. TELBIN.
A Room in a Village Inn,	Mr. PITT.
Parlour at Adam Brock's,	Mr. PITT.
The Ramparts of Stralsund,	Mr. THOMAS GRIEVE.
Old Tapestry Chamber,	Mr. LOUIS HAGHE.
Another Chamber,	Mr. PITT.
Hall of Audience,	Mr. PITT.

To conclude with, (twenty-third time) an original Farce, in One Act, by Mr. CHARLES DICKENS and Mr. MARK LEMON, entitled

MR. NIGHTINGALE'S DIARY.

Mr. NIGHTINGALE,	Mr. FRANK STONE, A.R.A.
Mr. GABBLEWIG, (of the Middle Temple)	
CHARLEY BIT, (a Boots)	
Mr. POULTER, (a Pedestrian and Cold-Water Drinker)	Mr. CHARLES DICKENS.
CAPTAIN BLOWER, (an Invalid)	
A RESPECTABLE FEMALE,	
A DEAF SEXTON,	
TIP, (Mr. Gabblewig's Tiger)	Mr. AUGUSTUS EGG, A.R.A.
CHRISTOPHER, (a Charity Boy)	
SLAP, (professionally Mr. Flormiville—a Country Actor)	Mr. MARK LEMON.
Mr. TICKLE, (Inventor of the celebrated Compounds)	
A VIRTUOUS YOUNG PERSON IN THE CONFIDENCE OF "MARIA"	
LITHERS, (Landlord of the "Water Lily")	Mr. WILKIE COLLINS.
ROSINA,	Miss FANNY YOUNG.
SUSAN,	Mrs. COE.

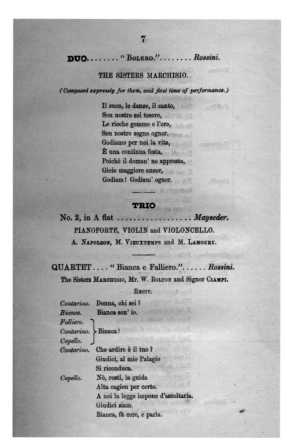

7

DUO........ "BOLERO."....... *Rossini.*

THE SISTERS MARCHISIO.

(Composed expressly for them, and first time of performance.)

Il suon, le danze, il canto,
Son nostro sol tesoro,
Le ricche gemme e l'oro,
Son nostro sogno ognor.
Godiamo per noi la vita,
È una continua festa,
Poichè il doman' ne appresta,
Gioie maggiore ancor,
Godiam! Godiam' ognor.

TRIO

No. 2, in A flat .... *Mayseder.*

PIANOFORTE, VIOLIN and VIOLONCELLO.

A. NAPOLEON, M. VIEUXTEMPS and M. LAMOURY.

QUARTET.... "Bianca e Falliero.".... *Rossini.*

The Sisters MARCHISIO, Mr. W. BOLTON and Signor CIAMPI.

RECIT.

Contarino.   Donna, chi sei ?
Bianca.   Bianca son' io.
Falliero.
Contarino. } Bianca !
Capello.
Contarino.   Che ardire è il tuo ?
Giudici, al mio Palagio
Si riconduca.
Capello.   Nò, resti, la guida
Alta cagion per certo.
A noi la legge impone d'ascoltarla.
Giudici siam.
Bianca, fà core, e parla.

become an operatic superstar, performing across England and becoming a famous name as far afield as Italy, Spain and the USA.

The work being performed in Santley's first Liverpool Philharmonic Society outing, back in 1849, was Haydn's *The Creation*. Jenny Lind was one of the soloists and, as Santley became better known, they often performed together. In November 1863, she was back in Liverpool to sing in Handel's cantata, *L'Allegro ed II Penseroso*, and in Mendelssohn's *Elijah*. Both of these guaranteed box office successes were conducted by Lind's husband, Otto Goldschmidt. He was obviously a man who knew the value of his wife's name on a concert poster. The Society allowed Lind and Goldschmidt to take home all of the net proceeds of the second concert.

The Leader Steps Up

By 1865, Zeugheer Herrmann was not a well man and the orchestra's leader E.W. Thomas took over the baton as an interim measure. Thomas was already a permanent fixture in the City's musical life, having joined the Phil as leader in 1849. He was a stunning violinist, and when Mendelssohn heard him perform the finale of his *Violin Concerto* faster than he had previously ever witnessed it being played, the composer said: 'He has more "go" than half the violin players I have ever heard'.

Thomas was only ever a stop-gap and, in September 1865, Alfred Mellon was appointed Principal Conductor. The Society took the opportunity to economise slightly, paying their new man £150 per year – £20 less than Hermann had received.

Thomas went back to his old job as leader of the orchestra, a role he continued to perform until 1883 – an unrivalled thirty-four-year stint. Alongside his role with the Phil, Thomas ran a series of populist concerts through the winter, which helped the Liverpool Philharmonic players to augment their earnings. After Hermann's death in 1865, Thomas took the additional responsibility of chorus master. There is no doubt that he was a brilliant musician and his presence in the orchestra helped the Society to persuade other major players to join up on a permanent basis.

Adelina Patti, described by Verdi as the greatest singer he ever heard.

The programme entry for the première of Rossini's duet *Bolero*, 7th January 1862.

The Liverpool-born baritone Charles Santley.

Jenny Lind, the 'Swedish Nightingale'.

Alfred Mellon

Born: Birmingham, 1820
Died: 1867
Principal Conductor: 1865-1867

Mellon was a man of many talents in his day: a brilliant violin player, a popular conductor and a well-known composer. As a player, he was the leader of the ballet at the Royal Italian Opera, Covent Garden. He became well known wielding the baton at London's Haymarket and Adelphi theatres and organised a series of Promenade Concerts in Covent Garden. As a composer, the opera *Victorine* was one of his most notable works. He was given the job as Liverpool's Principal Conductor in September 1865, but died just eighteen months later. He was buried in Brompton Cemetery in London, under an extraordinarily grand monument. By all accounts, his was a popular appointment and his death robbed the orchestra of a conductor who might well have developed their concerts along a totally new pathway.

Sir Julius Benedict

Born: Stuttgart, 1804
Died: 1885
Principal Conductor: 1867–1880

Julius Benedict moved in esteemed musical circles and studied under the composers Hummel and Weber. In 1822, he accompanied Weber to Vienna and was introduced to both Beethoven and Schubert, even dining with Weber at Beethoven's table in Baden. Two years later, Weber wrote a letter to Benedict's father saying: 'If God grants Julius the perseverance and modest humbleness of the true artist ... he cannot fail to achieve considerable success'. In 1825, Benedict was made music director of the San Carlo and Fondo theatres and it was here that he became friendly with the composers Paganini, Bellini, Donizetti and Rossini. Five years later, he moved to Paris. There, his friends included Berlioz, Chopin and Liszt. In 1850, he accompanied Jenny Lind as her pianist on her tour of the USA. Benedict became increasingly well-known in England, conducting every Norwich Festival from 1845 to 1878. He composed sixteen overtures, three piano concertos, two symphonies, eighteen violin sonatas, one hundred songs, four operas and more than eighty solo piano works.

Autograph of Clara Schumann, distinguished pianist and composer, and widow of Robert Schumann.

Autograph of Arthur Sullivan, who appeared on a number of occasions at Liverpool Philharmonic Society concerts.

Autograph of Charles Gounod, who conducted his own *St Cecilia Mass* at Philharmonic Hall.

Series of Three
of the London
"Monday" Popular Concerts
First Concert, Wednesday 4th Jany
1869

Clara Schumann

Concert
Tuesday 15 March 1870
"The Prodigal Son"
Conducted by the Composer
Arthur S. Sullivan

Concert
Tuesday 21 March 1871
"Messe Solennelle"
Conducted by the Composer.
Charles Gounod

Happy Days

Julius Benedict was well-connected and a big name for the Society. He signed up for the job on the same terms as Alfred Mellon and stayed in the role for twelve years, only leaving because of his failing eyesight. Born in Germany, he took British citizenship and was knighted in 1871. He spoke perfect English but retained his heavy German accent and eyebrows were raised on one occasion when he exhorted members of the choir to pronounce more clearly the words to 'O for ze vinks off a duff'.

Although the final decisions on concert programmes lay firmly with the Society's committee, Benedict does appear to have enjoyed greater influence than his predecessors. For the first time, concertgoers were able to learn about the composers and the works they were hearing in the printed programmes, known at the time as the 'Book of Words'. Written by Benedict himself, these essays gave the audience a far greater understanding of what was being played. In musical terms, Benedict can be credited with widening the orchestra's symphonic repertoire, and he also championed general improvements in the quality of the players. In 1872, the Committee noted 'the increased interest shown by the audience during the performance of symphonies and concertos as satisfactory proof of improvement'. However, one critic of the day wrote that the chorus had little to do except 'to set off, by the many-coloured attire of the ladies and the black coats of the gentlemen, the delicate cream and gold of the organ case and pipes'. Benedict's success in presenting symphonies was in contrast to his predecessors. There had previously been reports of members ostentatiously opening their newspapers when a symphony began.

In 1869, a new series of 'London Monday Popular Concerts' was launched. The name seems incongruous to us now, but at the time the 'London Monday Popular Concerts' that actually took place in the capital were a famous musical event and the Society must have hoped that some of the lustre of these weekly performances would rub off. The Liverpool performances were largely chamber music affairs and, despite their name, were not that popular at all, fizzling out a few years later.

As the orchestra strengthened, so did the range of composers it performed, with Benedict's concerts including Mendelssohn, Spohr, Beethoven, Rossini, Weber, Schumann, Bach, Brahms and Wagner. In 1870, Arthur Sullivan came to Liverpool to conduct his *Prodigal Son* and, in 1871, Charles Gounod visited the City to direct his *St Cecilia Mass*.

In 1876, the Phil's season changed from running through a calendar year to seeing the season launch in October with the closing concert in April. These days, the summer break is shorter, with the season beginning in September and finishing with the Summer Pops concerts in July.

As Benedict's eyesight became worse, his conducting became more and more uncertain. By the end of his career, performing in front of him must have been something of a gamble. To help him see more clearly, special lighting was provided for him. Unfortunately, it did little to help him keep the performance of Mendelssohn's *Athalie* together, as reported in *The Liverpool Mercury:*

> The work of those he conducted was continually jeopardized in consequence of the failure of his sight. An extraordinary pair of lamps had been rigged up for him at the rostrum, but they proved of only partial assistance and rendered more vivid with their glaring light the final episode of the regular career of the antique conductor of the Philharmonic Society … The whole went unsteadily, and more than once utter collapse seemed imminent. Matters grew worse apace towards the close of the performance, and the suspense at one portion was almost unbearable. It seemed there could be nothing less than a positive breakdown, but the veteran knew of a haven not far ahead, and heedless of the beats or bars he skipped, he gave an appealing look at the trumpets and trombones, which they were not slow to interpret, the chorus took up the cue, and with a triumphant shout at the words 'Heaven and Earth', one of the most painful recollections of half a century of music in Liverpool was brought to as painless conclusion as might be.

The 76 year old Principal Conductor realised his predicament and resigned. The Committee decided to give him a benefit concert, which earned him £300 to help fund his retirement.

In financial terms, Sir Julius Benedict's twelve years at the helm of the Liverpool Philharmonic had been very profitable. He had also benefited the orchestra just as much in artistic terms, leaving it in good health. Sadly, the orchestra's next Principal Conductor was not to have such a happy relationship with Liverpool.

Chapter Three

Mixed Reviews

Ian Bracken & Hilary Browning. Cellos, Royal
Liverpool Philharmonic Orchestra. Photographed at
the public artwork, *A Case History* by John King,
located on Hope Street, Liverpool.

LIVERPOOL.

PHILHARMONIC HALL.

THE FIRST

Harrison Concert

OF THE

SEASON 1902-1903.

FRIDAY EVENING, OCTOBER 24, 1902.

BOOK OF THE WORDS,
SIXPENCE.

Percy Harrison,
Concert Director, Birmingham.

J. UPTON, TYP., BIRM.

The Unhappy German

Max Bruch's first concert performance with the Liverpool Philharmonic Society was during Sir Julius Benedict's tenure, on 23rd October 1877, when he conducted the orchestra in his own oratorio *Odysseus*. It went down well with the critics. The *Musical Times* said:

> The attendance was large; the reception of the work hearty, and the whole affair gave Liverpool reason to boast that its new musical season has already accomplished no mean thing.

The *Liverpool Daily Post* also lavished praise on Bruch, describing the evening as 'an unqualified success':

> Both band and chorus acquitted themselves admirably under the able composer's baton, and it was satisfactory to note that the coldness which was apparent early in the evening gradually gave way to enthusiasm, Herr Max Bruch being loudly cheered at the conclusion of the performance.

Bruch was back in Liverpool on 18th November 1879, this time for a performance of his cantata *Das Lied von der Glocke,* which translates as *The Song of the Bell*. Again, Bruch wowed the *Liverpool Daily Post:*

> We cannot hesitate to affirm that Tuesday night's performance was one of the grandest achievements of choral singing ever heard within the walls of the Philharmonic Hall. Mr Sudlow, by his judicious and well-directed efforts to secure adequate rehearsals for Max Bruch's work, has undoubtedly given a stimulus to his choristers, which will … eventually place the choir in a position of second to none in England. Mr W.T. Best was an all-powerful aid on the organ … and showed a mastery, even over the wretched instrument he had to perform upon, unsurpassable by any living player!

The Committee Picks Their New Man

On 23rd February 1880, the Liverpool Philharmonic Society Committee decided on what they would expect from their new conductor. Their chief requirement was that he would live in the City during the concert season, rather than commuting up and down from London, as Benedict had been allowed to do. They were prepared to pay more money to get the right man, with the fee being agreed at £400 per year, with the expectation that the successful candidate would combine the role of conductor and chorus master. Thirty-three people applied for the job, including Frederic Cowen. The Committee decided to widen their search to candidates who had not actually applied, adding Charles Hallé, Alberto Randegger, Hans Richter and Max Bruch to the list for consideration.

Hallé, Randegger and Richter quickly ruled themselves out of contention because none of them was prepared to live for a large chunk of the year in Liverpool. Bruch's name stayed in the frame after he indicated that he would consider the move to Merseyside. Gradually the list of those who had applied was whittled away, until only Frederic Cowen and Max Bruch remained. In the end, the selection committee recommended that Bruch be given the job. The offer was confirmed and accepted in April 1880. Bruch insisted that he take on the role of piano accompanist, as well as being conductor and chorus master.

DAS LIED VON DER GLOCKE:

(THE SONG OF THE BELL)

GEDICHT
VON
FRIEDRICH VON SCHILLER,
COMPONIRT
VON

MAX BRUCH.

TRANSLATED INTO ENGLISH
BY
MRS. NATALIA MACFARREN.

Programme from Max Bruch's triumphant appearance at the Phil in November 1879, when he conducted his own work *The Song of the Bell*.

Max Bruch

Born: Cologne, 1838
Died: 1920
Principal Conductor: 1880-1883

Bruch enjoyed a long career as a teacher, conductor and composer. His *Violin Concerto No. 1 in G minor* remains one of the most popular of all violin concertos. For many years, listeners to Classic FM voted it their favourite classical work of all time in the annual *Hall of Fame* poll.

While he was in Liverpool, two of his works received their world premieres: his *Hebrew Melodies* (now known as *Three Hebrew Songs*) on 2nd November 1880 and *Kol Nidrei* (which has the subtitle *Adagio on Hebrew melodies for Violoncello and Orchestra*) on 7th February 1882. Liverpool also played host to the UK première of Bruch's *Scottish Fantasy* on 22nd February 1881. The violin soloist was Joachim, who was facing marital difficulties at the time. Bruch was not happy at all with the performance, blaming Joachim for ruining the night.

Liverpool may not have been an entirely happy time for Bruch on the work front, but it marked a very harmonious period away from music. Towards the start of his tenure in Liverpool, he became engaged to 16-year-old Clara Tuczek. By this stage, he was 42 years old and had had enjoyed a full and eventful private life. Some of his letters home to Germany describe the attention he had been receiving from the young ladies of Liverpool. Clara moved to Liverpool in January 1881 and they lived together in a large three-storey rented house at 18 Brompton Avenue, Sefton Park. Despite Bruch's reservations about her being anything other than a housewife, she acquitted herself very well singing Verdi's *Requiem* with the Liverpool Philharmonic in March that year. Their daughter Margarethe was born on 29th August 1882 and the register of births held by the Liverpool Record Office confirms that she was born in the Toxteth South area. So, although her parents were both German, she could claim to be a true Scouser.

Bruch Moves to Liverpool

Over the next three years, Max Bruch conducted 35 concerts with the Phil. He continued to enjoy a warm press from the critics, although his relationship with the chorus was every bit as prickly as that of J. Zeugheer Herrmann had been before him.

Although courteous, Bruch's letters to Henry Sudlow were often blunt. The Committee still had the final say on all repertoire and performers for the Society's concerts. On 6th June 1880, Bruch ended a letter to Sudlow, written in Berlin, by saying: 'I should prefer to fix the small Chorus and Orchestra pieces, myself, as the Committee does not know them.'

Bruch was supportive towards the orchestra throughout his time in charge, although that did not prevent him complaining about the behaviour of one or two individual players in letters to Sudlow. On 26th January 1881, he wrote:

> As to Jollyfe, the Tymbalist … it is a shame, really, that a member of our Orchestra does not come to the General Rehearsal, without making any excuse, and that tonight during the first part of the concert he was unable to play – evidently because he had drunk.

He returned to his theme in another letter to Sudlow on 2nd February 1881:

> Did Jollyfe send a letter of excuse to the Committee, or not? I have not received a letter from him, and find that he is a naughty man.

And again on 22nd February 1881:

> It is a very unpleasant thing indeed, that Mr Jollyfe is so deaf, and that evidently the instruments are not good. Very seldom the Kettle-Drums are in tune; the beginning of the Beethoven Concerto was really awful.

The tone of Bruch's letters to Sudlow gradually becomes more hectoring. On 18th November 1881, he told him:

> Our concerts begin too late, and the interval is too long.

By 19th July 1882, Bruch was exasperated with the Committee, writing:

> The Selection Committee, in their last meeting, did not accept my proposal, to offer an engagement for our first concert to Dr. Ferdinand Hiller. Allow me to say that I am seriously compromised against Dr. Hiller by this unexpected and very unpleasant decision.

Bruch was not afraid to criticise the work of his fellow composers. Charles Gounod comes in for a particularly strident critique in the same 1882 letter, with the solos in Gounod's *Redemption* being described as:

> … partly very nice … partly very monotonous and mediocre … it is my duty to say, that from the beginning to the end there is not one Chorus, which deserves to be called really a Chorus. They are, without any exception, very small, poor, and insignificant. There is also no independence of the voices; Soprano, Alto and Tenor and Bass sing always together – tone on syllable, – syllable on tone, in an almost incredible manner.
>
> That is not Choral music, – only Soprano Songs with added voices; Alto, Tenor and Bass have no other business, than to accompany the Soprano. I am sure that no English chorister, in the whole country, will agree with such an incredible and bad treating of the Choruses. If English or German authors composed such Choral music, they would be crucified – and surely, they would have deserved their martyrium!
>
> This is my opinion of Gounod's Choral music in the *Redemption*, and I need not say, that I am ready to defend it against everybody, even against the composer himself, if he would like to know my views!

The Liverpool concert attendees were not exempt from criticism from Max Bruch either. In a letter on 16th October 1881, he wrote:

> I recommend the Committee to take in consideration very seriously the insolence of a small minority of our public who are always talking awfully during the performance of instrumental works … I have been in the whole

Joseph Joachim
Since many years at the Philharmonic
Concerts.

— As to the Committee's
decision regarding the
performance of Gounod's
Redemption, allow
me to say that in my
opinion there is no
reason to decide a
question of such impor-
tance in a hurry.
It is the first time
that the renowned
and favourite Opera-
Composer has written
an Oratorio; I think
it therefore not only
most desirable, but
necessary, to post-
pone a definite
decision, until
the

2/
Birmingh. festival is over.
The fact is, that the
Birmingham Committee
and Mr. Gounod are
going to make an
experiment; and, so
far as I know the
opinion of the Birming-
ham Choir, this ex-
periment has not been
successful at all. —
After having examined
carefully the Vocal-
Score, my personal
opinion is, that the
Solo-pieces are partly
very nice (mostly
in the style of Gounod's
Operas) partly very
monotonous and
mediocre; — as to

To the Chairman and Committee of the Liverpool
Philharmonic Society.
We the undersigned, beg respectfully to request that,
prior to any steps being taken towards filling the office
of conductor rendered vacant by the resignation of Mr.
Max Bruch, you will convene an Extraordinary
General Meeting of the Proprietors of the Liverpool
Philharmonic Society, for the purpose of giving them
an opportunity of expressing their views as to the
future course to be pursued by the Society in
regard to the Subscription Concerts.
Pray inform us whether it is needful, by the Deed,
now to give the terms of any motion or motions to be then
proposed.
Liverpool 22nd January 1883.

of Germany, in France, in Belgium, Holland, Switzerland, and in the different parts of England, but I never saw that the minority offended in this way the large majority of the honest public, the artists, the conductor and the art itself.

The Committee responded swiftly by passing a new resolution on 17th October 1881, the very next day:

> … that Commissionaires be placed at each of the box corridors at the next concert, and that a printed slip be placed in each of the book of words.

The slip read:

> The Committee urge the support of the proprietors in maintaining silence in the Hall and Corridors during the performance. The Refreshment Rooms will remain open the whole evening where conversation can be carried on without disturbing the audience.

Time to Go

By the end of 1882, Bruch had decided that it was time to move on from Liverpool. As if making a New Year's resolution, he wrote his resignation letter to Henry Sudlow on New Year's Day, 1883:

> You will oblige me by communicating to your Committee, that in December I have received the offer of the position as conductor of the concerts in Breslau, the capital of Silesia and the largest provincial town in Germany, and that, after very careful consideration, I have come to the decision to accept this honourable offer. In consequence of this decision, I am now compelled hereby to give formal notice to the Committee of the Liverpool Philharmonic Society of my intention to terminate my present engagement on the 1st May next, in accordance with my agreement with your Society.
>
> Allow me, my dear Sir, to express through you to the Committee the sincere regret with which I leave my present position as conductor of

such distinguished a Society, but my intention having always been to return sooner or later to my native land, I could not refuse so favourable an opportunity, which might not have offered again for many years. I intend and hope to visit England frequently in the future, and I trust it may be my good fortune to keep up those friendly relations with the Liverpool Philharmonic Society which I value very highly.

The Committee's minutes for their meeting dated 22nd January read:

> That Mr Bruch's request be agreed to, it being understood that the cost of supplying a substitute for the last concerts shall be at the charge of Mr Bruch and that he be informed that the Committee may possibly ask for his assistance as offered.

> Mr Bruch also asked for the loan of some of his works to take with him to America. Request declined.

Before he took up his new job, Bruch had an American tour to complete. His final concert in Liverpool was Gounod's dreaded *Redemption*: the Committee had it their way right until the very end. Leaving his wife Clara and daughter Margarethe behind in Liverpool, Bruch set sail from the City on the Cunard steamer *Gallia* on 31st March 1883. Like so many of the famous names who passed through the port at the time, his destination was New York.

New Blood

As he sailed across the Atlantic, Bruch must have been thrilled to be visiting the 'New World'. Back in his old world, he had left behind an organisation that was on the verge of imploding. Morale – and the general standard of performance – had plummeted in the chorus; the orchestra was left rudderless without a creative dynamo to lead them; and the members of the Committee of management had begun to squabble among themselves about the best way to dig the organisation out of the hole it had got itself into.

On 22nd January 1883, a long list of the Society's proprietors wrote to the Committee:

> We the undersigned, beg respectfully to request that, prior to any steps being taken towards filling the office of conductor rendered vacant by the resignation of Mr Max Bruch, you will convene an Extraordinary General Meeting of the Proprietors of the

Liverpool Philharmonic Society for the purpose of giving them an opportunity of expressing their views as to the future course to be pursued by the Society in regard to the Subscription Concerts.

Conversations were underway between the Society and Charles Hallé to take over as the Liverpool Philharmonic's Principal Conductor, alongside his role at the head of his own orchestra based in Manchester. But before those negotiations could be concluded, there was an attempt at a coup on the Committee itself.

Other than the 'defalcations' of William Sudlow, life on the Committee seems to have been a remarkably staid existence up until this point. One G.R. Cox was the ringleader of the coup, ending up heading a band of eight new members on the thirty-two strong Committee. The Society's Annual Meeting in 1883 was adjourned and the Committee issued a statement against Mr Cox in May:

> The Committee (except the eight new members) ask the Proprietors to sanction the principle laid down in the Report, namely, that the Committee, and not the whole body of the Proprietors, ought to elect the Conductor. The Committee believe that the best Conductors will decline to run the risk of having their qualifications discussed in a public meeting, and probably in competition with the qualifications of others … It was intended to give the Society an opportunity of pronouncing upon a principle, namely, whether the Philharmonic Band should be discontinued and Mr Hallé's Band engaged instead? Whether that scheme was desirable to the Society or not, Mr Hallé has declined to enter into any such arrangement. There is therefore no question of principle left, but only the personal qualifications of various conductors – a matter which the Committee submit can be better dealt with in the committee-room than in general meeting. Mr G.R. Cox and his friends have now got eight representatives on the Committee, and the Committee are entirely unpledged to any particular Conductor at present.

Eventually, Charles Hallé was persuaded to take over as the Society's conductor. He was a truly great choice: a born diplomat, he quickly managed to unite the various warring factions in the Society, although there was still some pain along the way. Many members of the chorus had been singing with the Society for decades and it was felt that some of them simply were not good enough. After a process of weeding out the weaker members, around thirty of the original line-up remained.

Sir Charles Hallé

Born: Hagen, 1819
Died: Manchester, 1895
Principal Conductor: 1883-1895

Born Karl Halle, he later added an accent to his surname to turn it into Hallé and changed his first name to Charles, when he moved to England from his native Germany. Music was in the young Hallé's blood, with his father having been a church organist and director of the town of Hagen's orchestra, choir and chamber music society. Hallé was a fine pianist who became well known to London concertgoers. He spent time in France and counted the composers Cherubini, Chopin and Liszt among his friends. As a conductor, he made his name in the northwest of England, settling in Manchester in 1848. In 1853, he became Director of the City's Gentleman's Concerts and on 30th January 1858, the Hallé Orchestra performed its first concert, although 'Mr Hallé's Band' had been performing in the City on a more ad hoc basis through 1857. Hallé joined the Liverpool Philharmonic Society as Principal Conductor in 1883, a role which he retained until his death in 1895.

Britain's Oldest Orchestra

The conventional wisdom in classical music circles suggests that the Manchester-based Hallé Orchestra has the honour of being the UK's oldest surviving symphony orchestra, but the documents in the Royal Liverpool Philharmonic's archives suggest that the RLPO has a far stronger claim to this title than their colleagues in Manchester.

Musical historians do not dispute that the Royal Liverpool Philharmonic Society is the second oldest concert-giving organisation in the UK. Only the London-based Royal Philharmonic Society, which was formed in 1813, predates it. The RPS had its own orchestra, but this was disbanded in 1932.

Charles Hallé was not a completely unknown quantity to the members of the Liverpool Philharmonic Society. A brilliant pianist, he had performed at the opening of the Philharmonic Hall back in 1849. He founded his own orchestra in 1858, five years after the Liverpool Philharmonic's Committee papers show that it first engaged its professional band.

During his time as conductor, he seems to have enjoyed a far happier relationship with the members of the Committee than his predecessors had done. He had a good deal of influence over what was played and who was playing it. Gradually, he changed the make-up of the Phil's orchestra, introducing many players whom he also engaged for his orchestra in Manchester.

From the very start, the Liverpool Philharmonic had three distinct sets of players: the 'Metropolitan Talent', who were the big names from London earning the best pay cheques around the country; players based in Manchester, many of whom performed in musical events across the North West; and players who were either Liverpool born and bred, or who had been persuaded to live in the City on a permanent basis. Although there were amateur players in the orchestra at the start, by 1851, the Committee had ruled that 'no amateur shall be permitted to take a leading instrument in the band'. The annual accounts show that by 23rd February 1853, there were 51 professional players making up the Liverpool Philharmonic, all of whom were on annual contracts. There would have been additional freelance players brought in to top up this number whenever the repertoire demanded it.

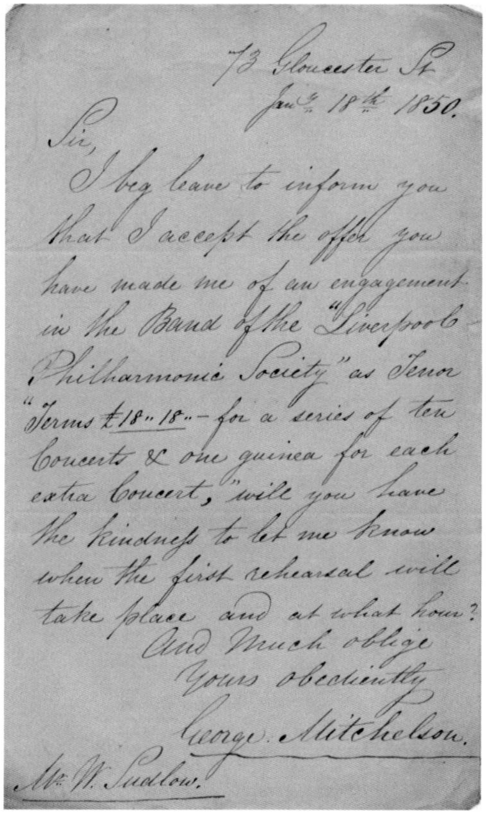

Letter 1 (top left):

> 73 Gloucester St
> Jan'y 18th 1850.
>
> Sir,
> I beg leave to inform you that I accept the offer you have made me of an engagement in the Band of the "Liverpool Philharmonic Society" as Tenor "Terms £18..18.." for a series of ten Concerts & one guinea for each extra Concert," will you have the kindness to let me know when the first rehearsal will take place and at what hour?
> And much oblige
> Yours obediently
> George Mitchelson.
>
> Mr W Sudlow.

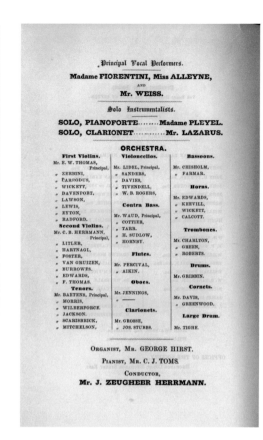

Principal Vocal Performers.
Madame FIORENTINI, Miss ALLEYNE,
AND
Mr. WEISS.

Solo Instrumentalists.
SOLO, PIANOFORTE........Madame PLEYEL.
SOLO, CLARIONET........Mr. LAZARUS.

ORCHESTRA.

First Violins.	Violoncellos.	Bassoons.
Mr. E. W. THOMAS, Principal,	Mr. LIDEL, Principal,	Mr. CHISHOLM,
„ ZERBINI,	„ SANDERS,	„ FARMAR.
„ CARRODUS,	„ DAVIES,	**Horns.**
„ WICKETT,	„ TIVENDELL,	Mr. EDWARDS,
„ DAVENPORT,	„ W. B. ROGERS.	„ KEEVILL,
„ LAWSON,	**Contra Bass.**	„ WICKETT,
„ LEWIS,	Mr. WAUD, Principal,	„ CALCOTT.
„ EYTON,	„ COTTIER,	**Trombones.**
„ RADFORD.	„ TARR.	Mr. CHARLTON,
Second Violins.	„ H. SUDLOW,	„ GREEN,
Mr. C. B. HERRMANN, Principal,	„ HORNBY.	„ ROBERTS.
„ LITLER,	**Flutes.**	**Drums.**
„ HARTNAGL,	Mr. PERCIVAL,	Mr. GRIBBIN.
„ FOSTER,	„ AIKIN.	**Cornets.**
„ VAN GRUIZEN,	**Oboes.**	Mr. DAVIS,
„ BURROWES,	Mr. JENNINGS,	„ GREENWOOD.
„ EDWARDS,	„	**Large Drum.**
„ F. THOMAS.	**Clarionets.**	Mr. TIGHE.
Tenors.	Mr. GROSSE,	
Mr. BAETENS, Principal,	„ JOS. STUBBS.	
„ MORRIS,		
„ WILBERFORCE.		
„ JACKSON.		
„ SCARISBRICK,		
„ MITCHELSON,		

ORGANIST, Mr. GEORGE HIRST.
PIANIST, Mr. C. J. TOMS.
CONDUCTOR,
Mr. J. ZEUGHEER HERRMANN.

Captions (right column):

Acceptance of terms by viola player George Mitchelson to play in the orchestra for the whole season in 1850.

Orchestra list for the concert of 23rd February 1853, the first time the Liverpool Philharmonic Orchestra was composed entirely of professional musicians.

Hallé's letter of 1883 saying he will try to persuade Brahms to come to Liverpool.

Autograph of Dame Clara Butt, the great British contralto.

Autograph of Australian soprano Dame Nellie Melba on a later appearance in 1901. One of the highest paid artists of her time, The Phil paid her £262 10s on this occasion. A decade later, the great Rachmaninov was paid £105 for his performance.

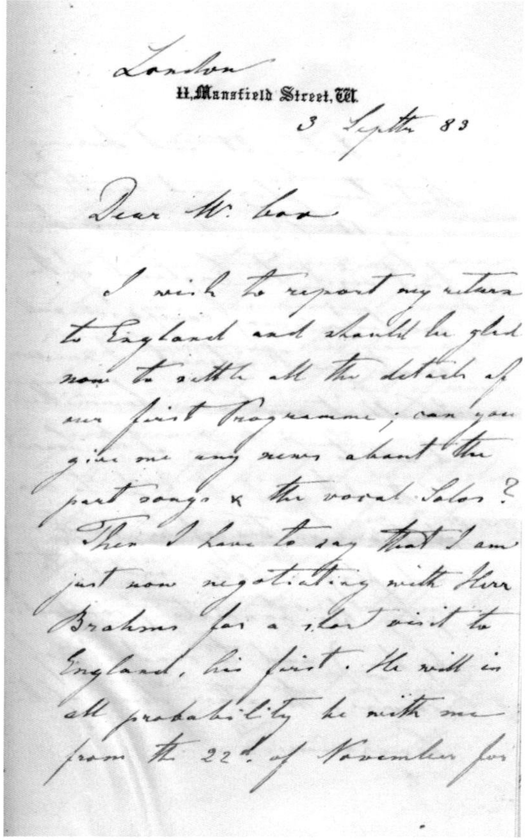

Letter 2 (bottom left):

> London
> 11 Mansfield Street, W.
> 3 Septbr 83
>
> Dear Mr Cox
>
> I wish to report my return to England and should be glad now to settle all the details of our first Programme; can you give me any news about the part songs & the vocal Solos? Then I have to say that I am just now negotiating with Herr Brahms for a short visit to England, his first. He will in all probability be with me from the 22nd of November for

7th Concert
7 January 1896
Season 1895-96

Clara Butt.

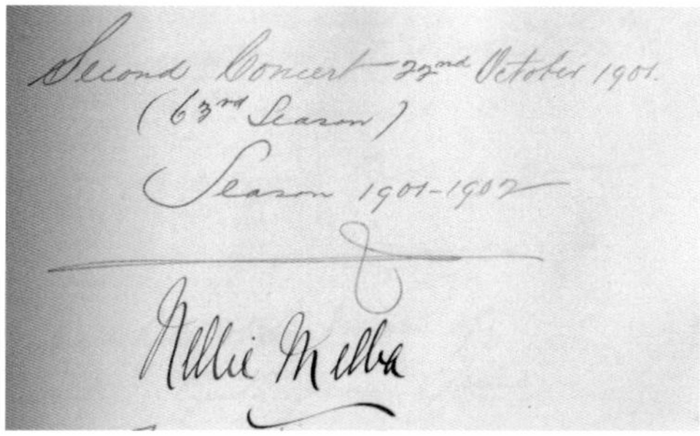

Second Concert 22nd October 1901.
(63rd Season)
Season 1901-1902

Nellie Melba

The Phil's archives contain several letters from players in 1850 accepting terms for that year's season. There is also a letter from W. Baetens, the Principal Viola player, dated 1851, which contains the following passage:

> The object of my writing is to convince you (if this is necessary) that
> Our Band, I mean 'The Phil of Liverpool' do not require so many
> Rehearsals than we had last year.

So, the Liverpool Philharmonic was an orchestra with a regular fixed rehearsal schedule and contracted players by 1851. By February 1853, not only were the personnel performing in the orchestra at the Liverpool Philharmonic Society's concerts contracted, but they remained relatively unchanged each season.

The theory that Hallé in fact took over the Liverpool Philharmonic and simply replaced it with players from Manchester is not borne out by a close analysis of the make-up of the Liverpool Philharmonic before, during and after Hallé's period in charge. True, in his second year at the helm, Hallé made drastic alterations to the Phil's line-up resulting in the two orchestras sharing a significant number of players. But, many of these came from outside the region altogether and were lured to the North West with contracts that allowed them to play in twice the number of concerts than would have been the case if they had a contract with only one or other of the orchestras. Throughout his time as conductor, the two orchestras had distinct identities. Hallé had himself refused to simply replace the Liverpool Philharmonic with his own orchestra before taking the Liverpool job. He was also allowed by the Liverpool Phil's Committee to bring the Hallé Orchestra itself to perform popular concerts in Liverpool, further underlining the separate identities of the two organisations. The two orchestras were never one single entity and after Hallé's death, the number of players performing in both orchestras was substantially reduced.

The repertoire of the two orchestras was also notably different, with the Hallé Orchestra leaning towards concerts that tended to be symphonic, whilst the Liverpool Philharmonic maintained its choral traditions, with repertoire from opera and oratorios featuring heavily. That is not to say that there were no symphonies to be heard in Liverpool; it was just that the audience seemed still to be slightly resistant to their charms.

Renewed Vigour

As Hallé set about restoring the orchestra of the Liverpool Philharmonic Society to its former glories, the new chorus master and pianoforte accompanist, Horatio Arthur Branscombe, was doing the same for the Society's choir. In a further change to the Society's line-up of key players, the Secretary Henry Sudlow died in 1883. His place was taken by George Broadbent, who stayed in the job through until 1909.

In a letter written on 3rd September 1883, Hallé sets out plans for his first season with the Phil:

> I wish to report my return to England and should be glad now to settle all the details of our first Programme; can you give me any news about the part songs and the vocal solos?
>
> Then I have to say that I am just now negotiating with Herr Brahms for a short visit to England, his first ... That this first visit to England of the greatest living composer will create great interest I am sure.

Although Hallé offers to arrange for Brahms to perform in Liverpool in December that year, his visit never actually happened. That did not stop Hallé from programming his music, with his *Symphony No. 2* being performed in February 1884 and his *Symphony No. 3* eight months later. His *Symphony No. 4* received its first Liverpool outing in 1887. Both the third and fourth symphonies were heard in the City a matter of months after their publication. Hallé was beginning to make his mark on Liverpool's musical tastes, by regularly programming unfamiliar symphonic works.

Famous names continued to appear at the Philharmonic Hall: Paderewski made his debut in 1890; the man who composed *Jerusalem*, Hubert Parry, conducted his now almost forgotten oratorio *Judith* in 1891; and the international soprano sensation Nellie Melba sang with the orchestra in 1893.

Another big voice of the time, Clara Butt, also performed at the Phil, as remembered by fellow singer, Laura Haworth Thraves:

Paderewski, the pianist who became Prime Minister of Poland.

71

I well remember Clara Butt's first appearance in *Judas Maccabaeus* at the Philharmonic. Trebelli's daughter was singing most of the soprano music, and I a smaller part. Trebelli did not arrive in time for the rehearsal, and Clara Butt was very anxious to try over one of the duets, so Sir Charles Hallé said: 'Madame Haworth knows this well, come and try it with her in the green room.' After the band had gone Sir Charles sat down at the little piano in that green room so familiar to Liverpool musicians, and Clara Butt, then a lanky high-spirited girl, sat on the table and boomed out the accompaniment with those phenomenal chest notes which became world-renowned. Sir Charles looked at her over the top of his spectacles, and said in his broken English: 'Vera gut, Miss Butt. Consider yourself engaged as my first trombonist for next season.'

When Hallé died in 1895 he left behind him a Liverpool Philharmonic Society that had improved fortunes, improved artistic credibility and an improved mood. The bad old days following Max Bruch's departure were now a distant memory, although the Phil was not exempt from criticism in the local press at this time. The *Porcupine*, a satirical magazine, devoted a whole column to the Society on 11th March 1893:

I hear that the committee of the Philharmonic Society have been taking lessons in the etiquette of costume; and as a result a violent amateur musician has been arrested in his progress to the stall of his adoption for not wearing a coat with tails. This is very terrible. It has, however, a compensating phase about it; for the suggestion is that if the committee of the local musical society are not able to give concerts that may be considered first-class, they are, at all events, alive to the fact that a theatre coat is not a swallow-tail, and that much injury is done to the social edifice by the admission to the sacred precincts of the Philharmonic Hall of a person clad in a garment that ends where the tail commences. That coats of this cut are accepted in London as being sufficiently full dress for public performances of a theatrical kind, is as nothing to the worthy magnates of our local society. They say in their lordly superiority, 'It may be the fashion in London, but it will not hold in Liverpool.'

While I am on the subject of the Philharmonic Hall I should like to suggest that the committee take some measure to stop the incessant chatter which occurs in the stalls. I have recently changed my seats in the hall, and I find myself in a hotbed of conversation that never ceases during the progress of the concert. If the means are not taken to abate this nuisance there will some of these evenings be a scene in the hall that will bring the importance of the matter home to the minds of the committee in a rather graphic way.

Sir Frederic Cowen

Born: Kingston, Jamaica, 1852
Died: London, 1935
Principal Conductor: 1895–1913

When Frederic Cowen was four years old, his father moved with his family from Jamaica to England to take up a position at Her Majesty's Theatre in London. The family travelled back to England via Liverpool. They stayed in the City for a few days, taking in a performance of *La Traviata*. The young Frederic was a prodigious talent, having completed the music for his first operetta by the time he was six. He studied piano with Sir Julius Benedict and by the time he was twelve, he could play several of Beethoven's sonatas. He composed his first symphony and piano concerto at the age of sixteen and his first large choral work *The Rose Maiden* was produced two years later. During a long career, he not only conducted the Liverpool Philharmonic and the Hallé Orchestra, but also the Bradford Choral Society, the London Philharmonic Society and the Scottish Orchestra (now the Royal Scottish National Orchestra).

73

Third Time Lucky

Frederic Cowen had lost out to Max Bruch when the Liverpool Phil's conducting job had been vacant back in 1880. He had also been overlooked when Charles Hallé was appointed in 1883. It is interesting to wonder what musical pathway the orchestra would have taken had it skipped over the unhappy Bruch years altogether by appointing Cowen instead.

In the fifteen years since he nearly got the job, Cowen had become one of England's leading conductors and was also a highly regarded composer. Initially, he took on the conducting roles at both the Liverpool Philharmonic and the Hallé Orchestra, which had been left empty following Sir Charles Hallé's death. However, within three years, he had been ousted from the Manchester job, to be replaced by Hans Richter. Here, the two organisations again showed their independence.

Richter was far the more conservative of the two conductors and under Cowen, the Liverpool Philharmonic gently trod a more contemporary pathway. Having said that, the concert programmes of the time featured plenty of Beethoven with a good smattering of Haydn and Mozart. The Society may still have been rather stuffy in its rules about who could attend and what they had to wear, but Cowen was prepared to blow away the cobwebs on the platform.

On 30th March 1897, he conducted the UK première of Berlioz's *The Trojans at Carthage*, and it was a big hit with the reviewer from the *Liverpool Mercury*:

> Mr Cowen is a musician who belongs to a high mental plane; he is eclectic to a degree, and one can easily fancy the readiness of his yielding to a desire to give *The Trojans at Carthage* a place in the repertory of the English concert room, a repertory which is even now not so rich in volume as it might be. In any record of his achievements which may appear hereafter, apart from the numerous works of his own which he has given us, his introduction to this country of one of the most notable works in the brilliant succession of Berlioz will be accounted to him as amongst the makings of history … Of the performance on this occasion there can be nothing but praise … the breadth of dignity and daring of Berlioz is

strikingly conspicuous. Characteristics of the treatment of the choruses by a fine body of voices were refinement, vigour, and a keen sense of rhythmical requirement, and the orchestra made plain their intelligence, judgement, and executive skill.

The Committee still retained the right of veto over Cowen's choices for each concert. In a letter dated 14th September 1897, to the Chairman John Wilson, he was particularly upset by the decision not to allow the performance of his latest symphony:

I confess to you that their [the Committee's] action in the matter has wounded my feelings in the matter very deeply. I am always the last to wish to force my own music on anyone, but as the Conductor of the Liverpool Phil happens also to be a Composer (who has worked hard to attain his position) I naturally concluded that the Committee would wish any new work from his pen to be included in their Programmes at the earliest opportunity, otherwise I should not have put it down without first consulting them.

Whatever may be the opinion of a few of the London critics, who by the way are antagonistic to nearly everything I write, I can conscientiously say that the work is one of my best or Richter would certainly not do it in Vienna, and even were this not the case, works by other English composers which are not up to their usual standard are included in the scheme owing no doubt to private influence, and this palpable rejection of an important work by their own Conductor has, I confess, come as a slap in the face to me.

I thought I should like to write to you a few lines, informally and not as Chairman, on the matter and if you could tell me the real reason for this palpable slight, it would be very kind of you. Please however, be assured that I have no wish to make a grievance of the matter. I am proud of being Conductor of the Phil. Soc. and have and always shall have its interests at heart as much as is in my power, and if I feel that it is the wish of the Committee that my position as Composer should be merged entirely, as far as their concerts are concerned, into that of Conductor, I shall accept that position without any further hesitation.

The Ascent of the Romantics

One English composer who was certainly making his mark in Liverpool was Edward Elgar. His *Dream of Gerontius* was performed for the first time in March 1903. This was certainly a braver move than it would appear to us now, as the new work was received abysmally at its première in Birmingham three years earlier. In the same year, Fritz Kreisler appeared in a performance of Bruch's famous *Violin Concerto No. 1 in G minor*. He had made his debut in 1902, playing Beethoven's *Violin Concerto*. Russian composers were starting to become part of the Phil's repertoire by now, with Tchaikovsky, Rimsky-Korsakov and Glazunov appearing in concert programmes.

The clamour for even more new music was loud from some quarters though, with one local critic describing the syllabus for the 1904-1905 season in less than favourable terms:

> Seasons come and go, the young folks of a few seasons ago are now men and women in their prime, heads that were brown are grey or bald, hearts that were blithe and gay have grown heavy and sorrowful; even the weather varies – for did we not have a fine evening for the opening concert? But still the Philharmonic Society appears to think first in arranging its concerts of how best to lead up pleasantly and without undue excitement to the greatly desired twenty minutes' interval, and then, of course, to the most effective way of declining towards the pleasant hour of 10.15, for which carriages may be ordered. Read down last evening's programme, and except for the date at the top there is nothing to indicate that the performance was not designed for a quarter of a century ago instead of for this year of grace 1904. How many times in the past ten years alone have we not gone through it all, just in the same order, and, to the credit of the Society be it said, with the same brilliant effect and artistic finish? Why, even the gentlemen who discuss grouse-drives and the prospects of pheasant shooting are beginning to know

THE

TWELFTH CONCERT

WILL TAKE PLACE ON

Tuesday, 30th March, 1897,

AT WHICH WILL BE PERFORMED,

(For the first time in England,)

"THE TROJANS AT CARTHAGE."

By HECTOR BERLIOZ.

———

Vocalists:

Madame MARIE DUMA.

Mrs. KATHARINE FISK.

Miss GERTRUDE IZARD.

Mr. HIRWEN JONES.

Mr. NORMAN SALMOND.

AND

Mr. EDWARD LLOYD.

———

Conductor:

MR. FREDERIC H. COWEN.

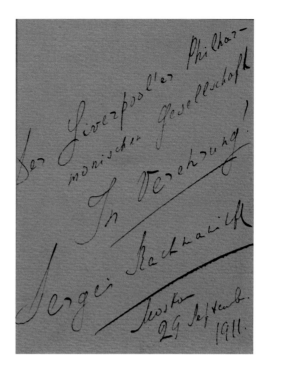

TELEPHONES :— { OFFICE. 3934 BANK.
HALL, 1904 ROYAL.

Liverpool Philharmonic Society Limited.

———

SEASON 1911-1912.

SECOND CONCERT,

TUESDAY, 24th OCTOBER, 1911.

CONDUCTOR—

M. RACHMANINOFF.

PROGRAMME.

———

Part I.

CHORUS ...	"Welcome Spring" (Nos. 1, 2 and 11) ... *(With Orchestra.)*	*Schubert*
ARIA	"Una voce poco fa" (*Il Barbiere*) ... Miss MIGNON NEVADA.	... *Rossini*
PIANOFORTE CONCERTO No. 3 (Op. 30) ...	*(First time in Liverpool.)* M. RACHMANINOFF.	*Rachmaninoff*

INTERVAL.

Part II.

SYMPHONY in E minor	I.—Largo : Allegro moderato. II.—Allegro molto : meno mosso. III.—Adagio. IV.—Allegro vivace. *(First time in Liverpool.)*	...*Rachmaninoff*
RECIT. AND POLONAISE ... "Je suis Titania" (*Mignon*) ... Miss MIGNON NEVADA.		*Thomas*
FANTAISIE	"Une nuit sur le mont chauve" ... *(First time in Liverpool.)*	*Moussorgsky*

The Concert will commence at a Quarter to Eight precisely.

910.]

Advertisement for the première of Berlioz's *The Trojans at Carthage*.

Dedication by Rachmaninov to the Liverpool Philharmonic on his first appearance in 1911.

The programme of the concert in which Rachmaninov made his Liverpool debut as both conductor and soloist in 1911.

Right: The great Spanish violinist and composer, Pablo Sarasate, who made several appearances at Philharmonic Hall.

Below. Another great violinist who appeared frequently was Fritz Kreisler.

Below right. Rachmaninov, who played at Philharmonic Hall and Central Hall in Liverpool.

Beethoven when they hear him between their loudly whispered confidences, though no doubt they would converse quite as comfortably through the strains of any other composer.

It seems that the sense of conservatism was not just limited to what was happening up on the platform. The Society had its rules and, however complicated they were, in the view of the Committee, they were there to be enforced. This notice was handed to concertgoers in October 1906:

> The attention of Proprietors, and those who **rent** Boxes or Stalls, is requested to the following Regulation which will be strictly enforced.
>
> No gentleman above twenty-one years of age residing or carrying on business in Liverpool, or within ten miles thereof, and not being an Officer of the Army or Navy, or Minister of Religion, is admissible to the Boxes or Stalls at the Philharmonic Society's Concerts unless he be a Proprietor, a member of the family residing at the house of a Proprietor, or has his name upon the List of Gentlemen having the **entrée** exhibited in the corridors.
>
> Resident Gentlemen, who are not Proprietors can acquire the right of Purchasing Tickets, or of making use of Proprietors' Tickets during the Season, by payment of an Entrance Fee of 10s. 6d.
>
> N.B. – Gentlemen above twenty-one years of age, although members of the Family residing in the house of those who **simply rent** Boxes or Stalls, are only admissible after payment of the Entrance Fee.

Behind the scenes, W.J. Riley was appointed as the Society's secretary following the death of George Broadbent in 1909. Broadbent had been secretary for twenty-five years and had been a huge force for good in the Society's life. Riley was to stay in the job for the next three decades. He would see the organisation through difficult times, including the First World War.

In 1911, Rachmaninov made his first visit to Liverpool, playing his *Piano Concerto No. 3*, and his *Preludes in C sharp minor* and *G minor*, as well as conducting his *Symphony in E minor* – a heavy workload for one performer, and something that the classical music stars of today would struggle to match. The critics were enthralled:

> It is exceedingly fitting to at once compliment the committee of the Philharmonic Society on the magnificent success, from the standpoint of music, which attended their second concert last night. It affords abundant proof of the wisdom of the forward policy which they have adopted, and if we mistake not we see signs of an awakening interest in the welfare of the Society which must make for the general good. On this occasion the committee undoubtedly placed the subscribers under a deep debt of gratitude for bringing to Liverpool for the first time the eminent Russian composer and pianist, Sergius Vassilevich Rachmaninoff, whose personality was reflected in fully three parts of the programme, for not only were two of his finest works introduced to this city, but he fulfilled a double duty – conductor and solo pianist. In the important part he thus played, Rachmaninoff seemed unconsciously to shed an effulgence on the concert, which received added glories as it proceeded.

> We in the City knew comparatively little of Rachmaninoff's music up to last night; that little may be summed up in the two characteristic Precludes [sic] – the more popular C sharp minor and the G minor; but one could not fail to realise, after hearing the two extended orchestral works now heard here for the first time, how great has been our loss.

The Rodewald Concert Society

The Rodewald Concert Society was formed in 1911 in memory of Alfred E. Rodewald, the celebrated Liverpool-based benefactor and conductor. The Rodewald Concert Society has been responsible for bringing some of the world's finest chamber musicians to Liverpool. Re-formed in 1998, the RCS now promotes an annual series of chamber concerts in partnership with the Royal Liverpool Philharmonic. The series is currently presented in the St George's Hall Concert Room.

The magnificently refurbished St George's Hall Concert Room is now the venue for many Rodewald Concert Society chamber music events.

The great Italian coloratura soprano, Luisa Tetrazzini, who signed this photograph on her visit to Liverpool in 1910.

As usual, there were still some critics of the Society at large in the City and some of the older concertgoers liked concerts to be the way they had always been. In 1912, one Society member decided to print a protest against the way some parts of the audience behaved during a performance of Elgar's *Violin Concerto* and *Symphony No. 1*. Although both of these works would be perfectly normal fare for an English symphony orchestra today, it is important to remember that this was 'new' music in 1911.

Signing himself 'Optimist Member', the pamphlet reads:

> We had first the Elgar Violin Concerto, an elaborate work taking up nearly an hour in its performance, and this was followed very soon by the Elgar 1st Symphony, another lofty work which occupied about the same length of time. The result was deplorable. The strain of listening for 180 minutes to two such high class works proved too much for the audience. During the Symphony the body of the Hall emptied visibly, and those who remained indulged in unrestrained and noisy conversation, so much so, that complaints the next day were noted in the daily Press.

Sir Frederic Cowen was ill for some months in 1911. His place on the rostrum was taken by Henry Wood and Thomas Beecham – two names of which we will hear more, later.

Once he was able to take up his baton again, Cowen remained in demand as a conductor across the country and in 1913 he resigned from the Royal Liverpool Philharmonic to concentrate on his other work. During his eighteen years in charge, he had succeeded in developing the Phil's concert repertoire to include many newly composed works and had also instilled a real sense of discipline in the orchestra. It was to be another twenty-nine years before the Liverpool Philharmonic Society would once again have a single Principal Conductor. The era of the Guest Conductor was about to begin.

A 'Brain Reeling' Idea

At the end of 1913, the *Liverpool Courier* reported a licensing hearing at which the Repertory Theatre applied for a music hall licence and the Philharmonic Hall applied for a cinema licence. The licensing hearing appears to have been knock-about stuff, which gives some insight into the social niceties of the time and bears repeating in full here:

A Classical Entertainment!

Mr T.J. Piggott, manager, made the application for a music hall licence on behalf of the Repertory Theatre.

The Stipendiary – That doesn't sound very elevating for the Repertory Theatre, does it?

Mr Piggott – Well, the idea is to hold Tango teas.

The Stipendiary – The Repertory Theatre and Tango tea! (Laughter).

Mr Piggott – Only in the afternoon, sir.

The Stipendiary – But the brain reels at the idea of Tango teas in the Repertory Theatre. What are Tango teas? (Laughter).

Mr Piggott – It means that people take tea while an artiste dances a dream dance on the stage. The same sort of performance has been given at the Empire and the Adelphi Hotel and we simply want to be on the same footing as the other theatres.

The Stipendiary – Well, it doesn't seem quite fair that you should not be put on the same footing as the other theatres. Personally, I should have thought that the Repertory Theatre would not have turned to Tango teas, but they know their own business, I suppose.

Mr Piggott – It is a classical sort of entertainment. (Laughter).

The Stipendiary – We grant you the licence expressing the pious hope that you will not have any more tango teas than you can help. (Laughter).

Desecrating the Philharmonic

The application in the case of the Philharmonic Hall was made by Mr W.J. Riley, secretary of the Philharmonic Society, who asked for a cinematograph licence. He explained that it was intended to hold an exhibition of moving pictures there for a fortnight, and that the display would be given by a London company which had rented the hall.

The Stipendiary – The whole world seems to be turning upside down. We have learnt that the Repertory Theatre is going in for Tango teas, and now the Philharmonic wants to turn itself into a picture palace. (Laughter).

Mr Richard Rutherford (one of the magistrates) – We shall be having the Cathedral making an application next. (Laughter).

Mr Riley said it was intended to exhibit one long film entitled 'Antony and Cleopatra'.

The Stipendiary – Is there anything so particularly elevating in the history of Antony and Cleopatra that the Philharmonic Hall should be chosen for its exhibition? We must have some justification for this application. The Philharmonic Hall is a beautiful hall, built for a special purpose. Why do you want to put it to this use?

Mr Riley – It means income to us.

The Stipendiary – But surely the Philharmonic Society can do without an income from picture shows.

Mr Riley – Frankly, the object of our letting the hall is to reduce our deficit at the bank.

The Stipendiary – A very laudable object, no doubt.

An objection to the application was laid by the manager of a Picturedrome in Myrtle Street on the ground of unfair competition.

The Stipendiary – I think you are entitled to object, and, to speak quite frankly, it seems rather a desecration that the Philharmonic Hall should turn itself into a picture palace.

Committee's Explanation

Mr Behrens, a member of the Philharmonic Committee, went into the witness box to explain the position. He was personally opposed to the idea of picture shows at the Philharmonic, but there were two points of view to be considered. The committee, after all, were only trustees for the shareholders, and the letting of the hall provided a substantial part of the revenue.

The Stipendiary said it seemed rather a hardship for these people, who held licences all the year round, and worked hard for the public, that as soon as Christmas came, when people were ready to spend a little more money, the Philharmonic should step in and ask for an occasional licence.

Mr Behrens – Of course the class of people who would go to the Philharmonic is not the same class as would go to the smaller halls. The prices would be higher for one thing.

The manager of the Myrtle Street house objected to this statement, and said plenty of people came into his show in evening dress after they came out of the Philharmonic. (Laughter).

The licensee of the Clayton Square Picturedrome also objected, and said he got as good a class of people at his hall as they would ever get at the Philharmonic. (Laughter).

The application was unanimously refused.

Chapter Four

The Big Names Come to Town

Alan Pendlebury. Principal Bassoon, Royal Liverpool
Philharmonic Orchestra. Photographed on the
Liverpool waterfront.

TELEPHONES :— { OFFICE, 3934 BANK.
HALL, 1904 ROYAL.

Liverpool Philharmonic Society Limited.

SEASON 1923-1924.

TENTH CONCERT,

TUESDAY, 11th MARCH, 1924.

CONDUCTOR :

Sir EDWARD ELGAR.

PROGRAMME.

Estimated times.

Part I.

OVERTURE in D minor ... ...*Arranged by Sir Edward Elgar.*	...**Handel**	4 min.
SONGS ... ... { (a) "In Haven" ... (b) "Where Corals lie" (c) "The Swimmer" ... } (*Sea Pictures*) **Elgar** Miss OLGA HALEY.		12 "
SYMPHONY No. 2 in E flat (Op. 63) ... ...**Elgar**		53 "

INTERVAL.

Part II.

... ...nd Orchestra) ... **Ernest Austin** 30 "

Liverpool at War

The resignation of Sir Frederic Cowen marked the start of a three decade period in the Liverpool Philharmonic's history in which many of the most highly renowned international conductors streamed into the City to conduct the orchestra. These included Rachmaninov, Elgar, Furtwängler, Szell, Monteux, Koussevitsky, Mengelberg and Walter. Alongside them, two of the most distinguished British conductors of the age, Sir Henry Wood and Sir Thomas Beecham, were also regular visitors to the Phil. The conductors joined an illustrious list of soloists and singers who came to Liverpool during this period. The roll call includes Pablo Casals, Lauritz Melchior, John McCormack, Elizabeth Schumann, the 15-year-old Yehudi Menuhin, Cortot, Solomon, Moiseiwitsch, Maggie Teyte, Busoni and Elena Gerhardt.

Unsurprisingly, the advent of the First World War in 1914 resulted in the complete absence of German performers at the Phil. There was never a time when music composed by Germans disappeared altogether, but there was a marked reduction in the number of German works being performed. There tended to be a greater focus on British composers, with an increased interest in music from the other Allied countries, including Russia and France. There was a notice in some of the wartime concert programmes warning that if there was 'sudden diminution or interruption of the regular lighting', attendants had been issued with 'hand electric lamps' to help concertgoers leave the building safely.

On 9th September 1914, the Society's Chairman, W.E. Willink, wrote to Members about the decision to continue with concerts despite the war:

> In preparation for the season's work, a number of Contracts have been
> entered into with Musicians and Conductors amounting altogether to
> some thousands of pounds, for which we should undoubtedly be liable
> whether the Concerts are held or not, seeing that we cannot plead *force
> majeure*. Even supposing that, if we decided against holding the
> concerts, we were able to obtain a substantial reduction in the amount

payable to these performers, it is clear that by this action, we should only be accentuating the financial loss, in many cases very serious, which has already been caused to Musicians by the unsettled state of things due to the war.

In our case the fact that a large proportion of the orchestra belong to the locality appears to us to be an additional reason for wishing to avoid the infliction of unnecessary privation.

The Committee would also like to point out that the Concerts which they provide are by no means to be regarded as frivolous social entertainments, the attendance at which would be inappropriate during a time of grave national anxiety.

The music which we endeavour to provide is serious in its character, performed and listened to in a serious spirit, and the Committee feel that they cannot charge themselves with any lack of proper feeling in offering to the public of Liverpool an opportunity of artistic enjoyment which they may be unable to find in other quarters. It is undoubtedly the fact that a large number of people in Liverpool will be engaged owing to the war in strenuous and often monotonous labour from which some relaxation is necessary, and if we, by holding our Concerts, can provide such relaxation, we shall be doing a work which is not only permissible but, even from the most patriotic point of view, advisable.

Unsurprisingly, anti-German feeling was high across Britain – and Liverpool was no different. An opinion piece in the *Liverpool Daily Post* in January 1916 penned by an anonymous 'Student of Music' was highly critical of the Liverpool Philharmonic's German former Principal Conductor:

Eight and thirty years ago there came to Liverpool to conduct the Philharmonic Society's concerts a third-rate composer from Germany named Max Bruch … I doubt whether 5 per cent of the present generation of the musical public could mention offhand the name of a single work which he ever composed … Bruch was a mixture of boor and baby: he was a

Second Concert
30th October 1934
"
Orchestral Concert

Very delighted of my first visit to Liverpool out of the Orchestra, which excelled itself —

George Szell

Philharmonic Concert
11th March 1924
"Symphony No. 2

Edward Elgar
Ernest Austin "Hymn of Apollo"
Olga Haley
Robert Joseffy
Jascha Heifetz

Above. Autograph book entry for the concert of 11th March 1924, containing the signatures of Elgar and the other performers. Rachmaninov, Jascha Heifetz and Robert Casadesus also signed the book.

Above right. Autograph of George Szell, who became famous for making the Cleveland Orchestra into a world-class institution.

Right. Autograph of the 15 year old Yehudi Menuhin on the first of his many appearances at Philharmonic Hall.

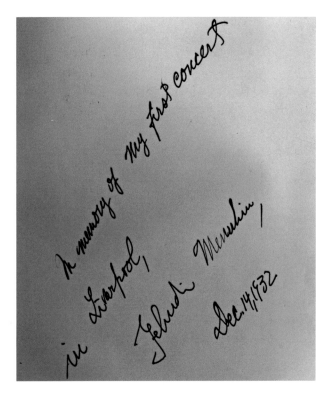

In memory of my first concert in Liverpool,
Yehudi Menuhin
Dec. 17, 1932

Left. Amelita Galli-Curci, one of the greatest of all sopranos.

Right. Pierre Monteux on his Liverpool debut in 1924.

Below left. Willelm Mengelberg, another of the great guest conductors who appeared at the Hall in this period.

Below. The great German lyric soprano, Elisabeth Schumann.

thoroughly incompetent conductor, having no ability to impart to his orchestra and chorus any artistic conception of the works he was performing; and his vile and childish temper made it impossible for any self-respecting body of musicians to tolerate his conductorship. His association with the Philharmonic Society lasted only three seasons and then he disappeared to the relief of everybody, leaving to that great gentleman and accomplished artist, Charles Hallé, the task of rescuing the Philharmonic from the rocks on which the German brute had left it.

Leaving aside the fact that Hallé was himself of German origin – something that appears to have escaped the writer's attention – this opinion piece sparked a considerable amount of interest in the newspaper's letters column. W.J. Bowden wrote:

> Max Bruch
>
> At the risk of being regarded as pro-German, I feel that the withering indictment under the above heading which appears in your issue of today must not be allowed to pass without protest. In the first place, no musician worth his salt would class the author of the *Violin Concerto in G minor* – which ranks with those of Beethoven, Mendelssohn and Brahms – as a third-rate composer.

The next day's paper carried a letter from F.C. Parr:

> I must heartily endorse Mr Bowden's most excellent and just letter. At the present time we are too prone to jump upon anything that happened to have its origin in Germany, either in art or anything else. This infamous and infernal war has nothing to do with music. Prussianised Germany is at present in the hand of the devil, but every broadminded and cultivated person ought to be able to detach their minds from this devils-inspired Prussianism when it comes to the discussion of art and artists, which is a thing quite apart.
>
> Max Bruch's greatest fault was his irascible, violent and uncontrolled temper, which at times made him behave as if he were bereft of his reason: but underneath that one found a man of downright sincerity and warm, deep affections.
>
> Through his uncontrolled temper he was the greatest enemy of himself, and he always did himself more harm than anybody else. When incensed he was capable of insulting his most intimate friend, and the next day sending a most touching letter

of apology. His unseemly and ungrateful remarks with regard to England the other day are simply the vituperations of an old man, with certain recollections, inflamed by his hot temper and poisoned by the corrupt press which prevails in Germany at the present time.

Although there were logistical difficulties in running the Society during the war years, there appears to have been no downgrading of the Committee's ambitions when it came to programming concerts: 1916 saw a performance of Granville Bantock's massive choral symphony *Omar Khayyám*. In the same year, Eugène Goossens III made his debut with the orchestra and the Chester-born conductor Adrian Boult appeared for the first time at the Philharmonic Hall.

As many as twenty-six of the Phil's players were on active service (although only one – E.G. Bennett, a horn player – lost his life) and it must have been difficult for the orchestra to meet regularly to rehearse. At the beginning of 1918, the Society gave a concert which included the choir and a selection of chamber works, but no full orchestra. The innovation was not one that was repeated with any regularity.

In 1915, the violinist Eugène Ysaÿe gave his first public concert at the Philharmonic Hall after his daring escape from wartime Belgium. His holiday home was in a seaside town a few miles north of Zeebrugge. As the German army advanced, he fled with his family by sea in a small fishing boat. It took nineteen hours in rough conditions to travel the thirty miles to Dunkirk. During the journey, they lost all of their luggage overboard. Ysaÿe managed to keep his priceless Stradivarius safe. Eventually, they crossed the English Channel and were given refuge in Tunbridge Wells in Kent. After a period of ill health, the violinist chose Liverpool for his comeback concert. He knew the Philharmonic Hall well and had, in the past, often attended concerts given there by his great friend, Fritz Kreisler. It goes without saying that Kreisler, an Austrian, would not have been a welcome visitor to Liverpool during the war.

The end of the war in 1918 did not seem to create as much of a stir at the Phil as might have been expected. In its usual understated way, the programme for the concert on 16th November simply asked the audience to join in singing *Land of Hope and Glory* at the end of Elgar's *Pomp and Circumstance March No. 1*, which opened the evening.

as the whole effect in 2ᵈᵉ movement (Intermezzo) depends very much upon this instrument. The Tenor Tuba or Euphonium in B flat (low pitch) is a very difficult & important part, in the first movement. it is rhythmically very difficult, & our player has played it many times, since the first performance at Queen's Hall from our manuscript parts. Is it not possible to engage him. Mr. Walter Reynolds (34 Florence Road, Stroud Green N.) if he could be secured I would only need him for one rehearsal on day or concert, the same would apply, if Mr. Souper was engaged as Bass Flute.

With all good wishes for the New Year

Faithfully Yours

Henry J. Wood

Between the Wars

The roster of visiting guest conductors was deemed to be a great success and it continued on throughout the period between the two World Wars. Each of the new stars who arrived in town created a buzz. Those who returned often, such as Sir Henry Wood and Sir Thomas Beecham, developed quite a following among the Society's proprietors.

These two men also did much to increase the orchestra's playing standards during this period. The expectations of the audience were also raised, with a greater amount of more challenging repertoire being performed more often. Gradually, the balance shifted away from choral pieces, which had been an absolutely rigid staple of the Society's musical life, towards more instrumental works. At the same time, the number of items in each concert was reduced, as fewer but longer works were performed.

In 1921, Sir Henry Wood conducted Rachmaninov's *The Bells*. The muddled handwritten Russian choral and orchestral parts made it a tough performance for the players and singers alike, but the conductor held the evening together and the reviewer in the *Liverpool Courier* described the concert as being 'undoubtedly the chief event of the Philharmonic season'.

The organ in the Philharmonic Hall had not been up to the job for many years and throughout the 1920s the Society fundraised for a new one. Against the backdrop of the depression, it took longer than anticipated to raise the money. One concert programme from the period includes an appeal for cash, pointing out that 'the organ is no longer in a state consistent with the high reputation of the Society'.

1928 saw a visit to the Philharmonic Hall by the Berlin Philharmonic Orchestra and their conductor, Wilhelm Furtwängler. They were given a warm welcome by the critics, including the man from the *Liverpool Courier*:

> The fame of this orchestra had preceded it, and it was expected on this, their first visit to Liverpool there would be a clamour for seats, as well as a great ovation for these German players. The one thing that impressed us most was the wonderful finish of their playing and the unmistakable way in which Furtwängler imparts his individuality to this force of nearly 90 players. This degree of finish is, of course, scarcely to be wondered at, remembering that they are playing together so often. Under similar conditions, no doubt, our own Philharmonic band would produce like results.

ACCEPTANCE OF ENGAGEMENT FOR CONCERT.

Contract with Sir Thomas
Beecham to conduct three
concerts with rehearsals in
1932 for the sum of £210.

Sir Thomas Beecham, Principal
Guest Conductor 1913–1942.

Programme for the English
première of Rachmaninov's
The Bells.

Wilhelm Furtwängler, who brought his world-renowned Berlin Philharmonic Orchestra to Philharmonic Hall in 1928.

Concert programme of the Berlin Philharmonic 1928.

Philharmonic Hall, c.1890.

TELEPHONES :— { OFFICE, 4582 ROYAL.
HALL, 1904 ROYAL.

Liverpool Philharmonic Society Limited.

SEASON 1928-1929.

THIRD CONCERT,

TUESDAY, 6th NOVEMBER, 1928.

AT 7-45 P.M.

BERLIN PHILHARMONIC ORCHESTRA.

CONDUCTOR—

DR. FURTWÄNGLER.

PROGRAMME:

Part I.

		Estimated times.
CONCERTO GROSSO in D minor (For Strings.)	... Handel	12 min.
SYMPHONY No. 1	... Brahms	42 ,,

INTERVAL.

Part II.

SYMPHONIC POEM	"Don Juan"	... Strauss	14 ,,
TWO NOCTURNES	{ (a) "Nuages" (b) "Fêtes" }	... Debussy	15 ,,
OVERTURE	"Flying Dutchman"	... Wagner	12 ,,

1094.]   The Concert will commence at 7-45 o'clock precisely.

The Great Evening Dress Debate

On 22nd June 1932, the Society's Secretary, W.J. Riley, sent a notice to members outlining the organisation's challenging financial situation. As the depression took its toll on Liverpool's rich merchant class, an increasing number of seats at the Philharmonic Hall were being surrendered. In total, 326 seats had been handed back over the previous thirteen years. The Committee was having trouble filling them and the Secretary proposed a radical solution:

> The Committee have given the question of Evening Dress their serious consideration, and are of the opinion that the position is such that a serious effort should be made to make the Concerts appeal to a larger public, and thereby obtain increased support, and they consider that this object might be more easily attained, and the Boxes and Stalls become more marketable if Evening Dress were optional.

For traditionalists, it was a disaster. The *Manchester Evening News* on 23rd May 1932, delighted in reporting the emotive debate under the headline 'Plus Fours Ban':

> Is evening dress, in some subtle way, conducive to the better enjoyment of a musical performance? Mr R.T. Golding, a member of Liverpool Philharmonic Society, thinks that it is, and he is also firmly convinced that an artist can perform much better if he has in front of him the immaculate white and black of men's evening dress. At the annual meeting of the Society in Liverpool yesterday Mr Golding objected to the suggestion that evening dress should be optional in the stalls and boxes, saying: 'We may not be Victorian, but let us continue to be Victorian and keep the atmosphere of our concerts.'

Not Snobbish

> In an interview with a *Manchester Evening News* representative today Mr Golding, outlining his views said: 'I do not base my argument on the idea that because a thing is, it always should be, neither am I a snob, but I maintain that if we allow somebody in fustian or plus-fours to sit in the stalls or boxes beside others in evening dress we are going to dissipate

the atmosphere of these concerts. The Liverpool Philharmonic Society is about 100 years old and is the one society in Liverpool at present carrying on the old good work in the good old way, and if we allowed evening dress to be optional in the boxes and stalls I think it would lower the dignity of the Society and its concerts.' Mr Golding saw in the ordinary clothes suggestion an attempt to bring into the Society the socialist idea. It had even been suggested, he said, that poor music teachers or school teachers should be allowed in the stalls at reduced prices to sit beside others in evening dress who had paid the full amount.

Resignation Fears

He thought such a policy, coupled with that on evening dress would result in greater loss by people resigning than in any gain through the filling of seats. If a person found he had not time to change into evening dress after his day's work Mr Golding suggested that he should go into the gallery, as he himself had done on such an occasion. Mr Golding also suggested that if a man had booked a box and found he could not change into evening dress he should be expected to sit at the back of the box. 'I think evening dress does help in the appreciation of music,' he said, 'and, speaking as an amateur musician myself, I know that an artist can perform better if he has before him what I can describe as a 'clean' audience.'

Fight to the End

If we allow optional dress we are going to bring the Philharmonic Concerts down to the level of board school concerts. The atmosphere created by evening dress is one of those things which, human nature being what it is, we cannot get away from, and so far as I am concerned I shall fight to the end to retain it.

The Committee conducted a vote among the membership, who were split down the middle. The Society concluded that there was not enough support to abandon the practice and Evening Dress continued to be compulsory. There were other restrictions on the Society, which we would regard as strange today. For example, it was forbidden to sell tickets at the hall on Sundays, although they were allowed to be sold in the vicinity of the hall. This led to one case where a cab was hired to parade up and down the street outside the hall selling tickets, as a way of legally getting around the ban.

Dreams Go Up In Smoke

At just after seven o'clock on the evening of 5th July 1933, smoke was seen pouring from the roof of the Philharmonic Hall, where builders had been working earlier in the day. The Fire Brigade battled valiantly, but the combination of fierce heat, rapidly advancing flames and thick smoke was too much for them. Quickly, the whole interior was on fire and the roof fell in. The *Liverpool Daily Post* reported that 'the dense crowds of watchers heard grim thuds as one portion after another fell within.'

The organ, which had been installed at a cost of £2,000 only three years before, was completely destroyed, but many of the hall's valuable artefacts were saved, including a series of autographs from visiting stars, some of which appear in this book. Hundreds of scores were carried from the music library to be stored temporarily in the Baptist Chapel opposite. Many of the orchestra's instruments, particularly the larger ones that tended to be kept at the Hall, were also destroyed:

> The blaze was so fierce that the heat could be felt in neighbouring streets, and passengers in the tramcars that passed alongside the hall before the traffic was diverted found the heat almost intolerable. The crowds that gathered were swept back by cordons of police as additional fire engines and tenders were rushed to the scene ... The blaze in the roof spread with great rapidity. The flames swept down on the firemen below, followed by an ominous crack and a rumbling roar as part of the superstructure crashed down near the men tackling the flames below. Meanwhile the blaze soared through the roof, with such menace to the firemen on top of the escape that the man directing the hose into the

burning building had to crouch beneath the parapet to prevent being scorched …
The interior of the building was soon a veritable inferno, and the brigade had to
concentrate their efforts upon the outside of the building. A small incident, but
one which illustrates the force of the flames that leaped from the hall, happened
when a pigeon, flying at a height over the burning building, collapsed and fell like
a stone into the flames.

The Hall was beyond repair and there was widespread sadness in the musical world. It had
been admired by many of those who performed there. Hans Richter described it as 'the finest
concert hall in Europe'. An editorial in the *Daily Post* underlined the tragic loss to the City:

> The disaster to the Philharmonic Hall cannot fail deeply to impress the imagination of the
> people of Liverpool and excite sincere regret among all classes. For one reason or other
> the hall had pleasant associations for most citizens. But it was its concerts which
> established its fame, and in that respect it had an interesting social as well as musical
> value. With the changing conditions, the social factor has naturally diminished in
> importance, but the musical interest has been on the whole courageously maintained. As
> our columns have from time to time shown, there are divergent views of the policy of the
> Philharmonic Society, but these are days of transition and the Society has striven
> earnestly to attract and hold the musical public. What will be the outcome of last night's
> disaster no one can yet say. It comes at a most awkward moment in the musical
> development of the City and sets a most anxious problem before the Society. It may be
> possible to refit the old structure and that will take time, and meanwhile Liverpool must
> be deprived of one of its most notable institutions. The whole community will sympathise
> with the difficulties of the Society, and the loss of the hall, whether it be long or short,
> will be very keenly felt.

The *Liverpool Echo* offered an interesting postscript to the fire in a column on 10th July 1933:

> Mr Robert Gladstone has been telling me some very interesting things about the
> famous acoustics of poor, burnt-out Philharmonic Hall. His father, he says, told
> him that he once met Cunningham, the architect of the hall, and asked him if he
> had any guiding principles in acoustics which had enabled him to produce such a
> perfect concert hall. Cunningham's reply was: 'No, I have no such principles; it was
> a perfect fluke.'

Firemen battling with the blaze at Philharmonic Hall, 5th July 1933.

The Hall on fire with part of the enormous crowd which gathered to watch.

Exterior of Philharmonic Hall after the fire which destroyed it.

Interior of the Hall after the fire.

Central Hall in Renshaw Street, where the Phil gave concerts from 1934 to 1939.

No Home of its Own

The Liverpool Philharmonic Society moved its concerts to the Central Hall on Renshaw Street. The conditions were not as good as those the orchestra had been used to enjoying, but it was a case of 'needs must'. The Central Hall remained the base for the next five seasons, although St George's Hall was used for large scale works involving both orchestra and chorus.

The long list of guest conductors continued to grow, with names such as Constant Lambert making their debut with the Phil during this period. Rachmaninov made a welcome return during 1935 to perform his *Rhapsody on a Theme of Paganini*.

Still No New Home

Everyone seemed to agree that a replacement for the Philharmonic Hall should be built, but there was considerable disagreement on exactly what it should be like; how it should be funded; and who should actually oversee the building. It took two years of negotiations and countless special meetings to arrive at a solution that was agreeable to everyone.

The old hall was insured and the insurance company had paid out to the tune of £84,000 for the hall itself, with a further £9,503 for other assets and £6,000 for the loss of two years' rental. The Society needed to negotiate the delicate issue of who exactly owned the old hall. After all, it was built by subscription and some of the shareholders in the Society believed that they could lay claim to partial ownership. In the end, the Lancashire Chancery Court ruled in July 1934 that the Liverpool Philharmonic Society's 'primary objective was the promotion of the science and practice of music, and the existence of the hall or a hall was entirely subsidiary to that.' In its ruling, the court 'did not think the interest of the members in their stalls and seats was a legal interest'. This judgement paved the way for a new hall to be built.

For a long period, it was hoped that the City Council would rebuild the hall in return for the Society surrendering its lease. Under the terms of the agreement, the Society would be free to continue to use the hall, although it would not own the

asset, as it had done before. After much debate, the scheme was shelved, not least because the hall that the Council wanted to build was to be a multi-purpose arts centre, rather than one that concentrated on classical music.

Sir Henry Wood was highly critical of the City Council's role and was quoted in the *Liverpool Daily Post* as saying:

> It is a crying shame to a city like Liverpool that it should turn down a proposal to provide a hall for its great Philharmonic Orchestra … The council which can do a thing like that must be composed of queer people. The Liverpool Philharmonic has done noble work in the cause of music, its influence cannot be over-estimated; yet here is the Council of its own city, which should do all in its power to help forward the musical cause, refusing assistance on the ground, apparently, that it would be a far better thing to provide a more expensive social centre.

> Music should not be mixed up with anything else. There are scores of places where people can dance and have their pizazz. Let Liverpool have its social centre, let the Council put it up for them but for goodness' sake don't make the fundamental and unforgiveable mistake of thinking that the cause of music would be served by simply allocating a bit of it to the Philharmonic.

> In my experience, serious-minded people are getting sick of the confusion of music with entertainment. Music is not entertainment. It is education in its highest sense; it is, if you like to express it so, uplift. If the City Council members cannot realise the difference, then they are out of touch with serious minds. Look at the Promenade concerts at Queen's Hall [in London]. They are attended by thousands of people. They prove, if proof were needed, that there is a huge and appreciative community of real music lovers, who do not want their enjoyment diluted by loathsome infusions of 'entertainment'. That community extends to Liverpool and is not the monopoly of London.

> I am told that one speaker at yesterday's meeting said the new hall would mean large expenditure to cater for the tastes of a very small minority of privileged classes. That is, of course, arrant nonsense. The success of the

Exterior of Philharmonic Hall.

Herbert J. Rowse, architect of the new Philharmonic Hall.

Interior of Philharmonic Hall.

Interior of Philharmonic Hall.

View of the Hall from the upper circle.

View of the Hall from the stage.

Promenade concerts is sufficient reply to that. Even if it were true, then adequate facilities for such important bodies as the Liverpool Philharmonic would turn the minority into an overwhelming majority.

Liverpool's decision distresses me, however, not only on account of its evidence of a lack of real musical sense, but also because it affects the general principle of employment. Music gives a livelihood to many people. Does dancing do that?

I feel strongly in this matter. It is dreadful to think that a city like Liverpool should deprive its orchestra of a lovely hall simply because its Council cannot see that if people want entertainment of the lighter sort they can go elsewhere.

In the end, the Society bravely decided to go it alone and to use the insurance money to rebuild the hall on Hope Street without assistance from the City Council. The architect, Herbert J. Rowse, was commissioned to design the new Hall. A highly respected local figure, he also designed the Liverpool architectural landmarks Martin's Bank, the India Buildings and the entrance to the Mersey Tunnel. In stark contrast to the classicism of the old hall, Rowse came up with an art deco design which was equally impressive in its own way.

In June, 1936, *The Liverpolitan* reported that the new building would be able to accommodate approximately 2,200 concertgoers and would cost around £88,000 to build. (As it turned out, the Hall would prove to be able to seat a smaller number of people and would cost rather more to complete.) A horse-shoe of private boxes surrounded the stalls seating, with a dress circle and gallery upstairs. The magazine notes that 'a feature of the design is that the boxes are planned to lie within the area of maximum acoustical efficiency'. The Hall was also to be equipped with projection equipment and a cinema screen and organ console that would rise out of the stage when needed. Herbert Rowse described the hall as being 'shaped like a megaphone with orchestra at the narrow end'. Parts of the foyer are said to be based on the decoration of the interior of Tutankhamen's tomb.

It had been hoped that the new Hall would be open for business by the end of 1938, but delays in finishing the building work pushed back the official opening to 19th June 1939. Sir Thomas Beecham conducted the opening concert the next day; the programme had been designed to show off the thoroughly modern acoustics:

Cockaigne Overture	Elgar
Two choruses from *Solomon*	Handel
'*Elizabeth's Prayer*' *(Tannhäuser)* and	Wagner
'*Leise, leise*' *(Der Freischütz)*	Weber
sung by Florence Austral	
Elegy for String Orchestra	Tchaikovsky
Oberon overture	Weber
Tannhäuser overture and *Venusberg* Music	Wagner
Andante and Finale from the *Organ Sonata*	Elgar
played by G.D. Cunningham	
'*Abscheulicher*' from *Fidelio*	Beethoven
sung by Florence Austral	
March from *Sigurd Jorsalfar*	Grieg

The minutes for the Society's General Committee on 17th June 1940 report the final costs for rebuilding the new Hall. Herbert Rowse had guaranteed that the total bill would not exceed £120,154. 4. 5d. Rowse himself would be paid a further £6,869. The Committee congratulated itself, saying it had 'secured a first class building at a moderate cost'.

The Organ

The new organ was built by the Liverpool firm, Rushworth and Dreaper. When it is not in use, it is easy to believe that the hall does not have an organ at all, because all of its workings are hidden away behind grilles on either side of the orchestra. The console can also be hidden away below the stage.

The First Concert in
The New Philharmonic Hall
Tuesday, June 20th, 1939
Price Sixpence

100th Season
1938-1939

Ninth
Subscription
Concert

Cover of the programme of the first concert at the new Philharmonic Hall, 20th June 1939.

The Philharmonic Hall's Walturdaw rising cinema screen.

Louis Cohen, who conducted the Liverpool Philharmonic on many occasions, and whose Merseyside Symphony Orchestra provided the players which allowed the Phil to survive the early years of the Second World War.

The Phil's resident cinema organist, Dave Nicholas, is an institution in his own right, and is pictured here in 2004 with former Chief Executive, Michael Elliott, celebrating fifty years in the business, including twenty years as organist at the Phil.

More than 120,000 yards of insulated copper wire were used to connect the console with the various sections of the organ. There are more than 17,000 switches and contacts in the organ, along with 2,847 electric magnets.

Today, the Philharmonic Hall's organ remains the oldest remaining working example of its type anywhere in the world. The same is true of the Waldurdaw rising cinema screen, which also remains in use today.

Liverpool at War Again

Just two months after the joyous opening of the new concert hall, Britain was at war with Germany once again. The effect on Liverpool's cultural life was far greater than it had been in the First World War. Evening concerts were abandoned; many people faced evacuation from the City; younger men were signed up for war work and it was far more difficult for players who lived outside the City itself to travel around. In October 1939, the Committee decided to resume Philharmonic concerts, as best they could. An emergency orchestra was formed, taking in players from the disbanded BBC Salon Orchestra and from the Merseyside Symphony Orchestra. This band had been formed a few years earlier by a Philharmonic violinist, Louis Cohen. It gave a series of popular concerts in New Brighton and on Sunday evenings at St George's Hall. At the same time, distinguished London-based players such as Henry Holst and Anthony Pini moved away from the capital to avoid the blitz and settled in Liverpool. Cohen was a tremendous force in the City's musical life and there is no doubt that without his endeavours, particularly at the beginning of the wartime period, the Liverpool Philharmonic Society would have struggled to continue.

Weekly subscription concerts began on Tuesday evenings under the direction of conductors including Sir Thomas Beecham, Sir Hamilton Harty and Sir Henry Wood. Louis Cohen continued to conduct the regular popular concerts and the young violinist Thomas Matthews was named as the orchestra's Leader.

AIR RAID PRECAUTION

In the event of an air-raid "Alert" taking place during a concert, the audience will know of such an "Alert" by the continuous burning of an amber light on the base of the Conductor's Rostrum.

Members of the audience may leave the auditorium if they wish.

As the music will continue without interruption, will those who are intent on leaving do so as quietly as possible.

Page One

Wartime programme telling the audience what to do in the event of an air raid.

Although the Phil's centenary season was subdued owing to the war, it still managed to include notable musicians in its line-up.

With no sign of the war coming to a close, the Subscription series was moved to Saturday afternoons for public safety reasons. The conducting duties were shared out between Louis Cohen, Sir Malcolm Sargent, Sir Hamilton Harty and Sir Adrian Boult. Members of the Armed Forces were allowed into the popular concerts and were offered subsidised tickets.

Liverpool was targeted by Luftwaffe air raids in 1940 and 1941, but the band played on despite the sustained bombing campaign. The minutes of the Society's General Committee on 14th October 1940 outline the way the Society would treat air-raids, which was either stoical or foolhardy, depending on your point of view:

> It was agreed that the Concerts should continue without interruption in the event of an air-raid alert sounding, and that the audience should be informed of this alert by the burning of an amber light at the base of the Conductor's Rostrum. Members of the audience may leave the auditorium if they wish. As the music will continue without interruption, will those who are intent on leaving do so as quietly as possible.

The concert programmes of the time also contained this note for disorganised concertgoers:

> Reminder – Do not forget to take away your respirator.

With the war at the forefront of everyone's mind, the Liverpool Philharmonic Society's one hundredth anniversary passed by without the fanfare that might have been expected in more usual circumstances. Sir Hamilton Harty conducted a special anniversary concert. It is worth pausing to note just how far the Society had come in its first century: in the 1939-1940 season, it gave a total of thirty-eight concerts made up of a subscription series of sixteen, along with sixteen Sunday and six Saturday popular concerts. This compares with its first year, when the Society put on a total of four concerts in a dancing saloon.

Chapter Five

New Hope

Blyth Lindsay. Tenor Trombone, Royal Liverpool
Philharmonic Orchestra. Photographed at Antony
Gormley's *Another Place* on Crosby Beach.

LIVERPOOL
PHILHARMONIC SOCIETY LTD.
109TH SEASON

Philharmonic Hall Liverpool

SYLLABUS
1947-1948

PRICE

SIXPENCE

A New Deal

With the war still raging, there was at least some good news for the Liverpool Philharmonic's finances, which had never been on the firmest of footings. The City Council agreed a new arrangement with the Liverpool Philharmonic Society, which saw the lease for the Philharmonic Hall being transferred to the Corporation [the City Council] on 1st July 1942, in return for a cash payment of £35,000 and an annual rent paid to the Society by the Council of £4,000.

In return, the Society was required to spend this annual income on 'the promotion of musical education in and around Liverpool'. This was defined, on an annual basis, as between sixteen and twenty-four concerts in the Hall; a further sixteen popular concerts with a pricing structure approved by the Corporation; and six education concerts. The Society was also expected to maintain a permanently contracted orchestra of at least 'forty-five instrumentalists preferably recruited from Merseyside residents.' The deal was brokered by the Phil's chairman, Sir David Webster, a key figure in The Society's evolution during this period.

On Disc

In December 1942, there was more good news reported in the minutes of the Society's General Committee – this time, on the subject of gramophone recordings:

> The basis was likely to be that we would conclude a contract with the Columbia Gramophone Company to record for them a minimum of six sessions during a year ... the H.M.V. Company [was] making a certain number of recordings in conjunction with the British Council, of modern British works. The first recording the Society would make would be of *Belshazzar's Feast* and the second, the Bliss *Pianoforte Concerto* with Solomon and Sir Adrian Boult. The fees for the Orchestra would be at the normal Musicians' Union rate. This agreement would last for twelve months.

> In connection with the recording of *Belshazzar's Feast*, it had been proposed by the British Council that a concert of William Walton's music should be given in the Hall on Saturday 2nd January 1943. The recording would begin on Sunday 3rd January. The Huddersfield Choral Society would provide the Choir. The programme for the concert would consist of:

Overture *Scapino*	Walton
Violin Concerto (Henry Holst, soloist)	Walton
The Wise Virgins Suite	Walton
Belshazzar's Feast (Dennis Noble, soloist)	Walton
Conductor – William Walton	

It was reported that the terms likely to be agreed would leave the Society £100 towards guarantee against loss. The Society would have no financial responsibility beyond the Hall and the Orchestra. It was agreed to proceed with arrangements for this concert.

The 1942-1943 season was a pretty momentous year all round for the Liverpool Philharmonic, with its first schoolchildren's concert in January, its first tour of North Wales at Easter and its first broadcast on the BBC in October. The Society's annual report at the end of the season noted:

> For the first time in its history the Orchestra played outside Liverpool. Last Autumn the Carnegie Trustees recognised the Orchestra as one of the seven National Orchestras of the country and guaranteed the Society against loss in promoting a number of concerts in towns within one hundred miles of Liverpool.

The first black conductor in the history of the orchestra appeared on 20th December 1942. Rudolph Dunbar, from British Guiana, was a virtuoso clarinet player who studied music in New York, Paris and Leipzig. Based in London, he reported during the war for a USA newspaper, which was read by thirteen million African-Americans. The review of his concert in the *Evening Express* was glowing in its praise:

> He established his right to a foremost place among our leading conductors … Musically the concert was a great success, and there was not a vacant seat in the hall. The highlight of the concert was Mr Dunbar's conducting of the *New World Symphony* of Dvořák. He showed inner understanding of this work which revealed fresh beauties. It was one of the best renderings of this favourite symphony that I have heard.

However, the biggest news of all was the appointment of Malcolm Sargent as Principal Conductor. He was the first person to have the role on a full time basis since Sir Frederic Cowen's departure in 1913.

GREATEST ARTISTS   FINEST RECORDING

"HIS MASTER'S VOICE"

Repeat the enjoyment of these splendid concerts—in your own home whenever you wish on

"HIS MASTER'S VOICE" RECORDS

Make a point of hearing the first records by the

LIVERPOOL PHILHARMONIC ORCHESTRA
Conducted by Dr. MALCOLM SARGENT

Tchaikovsky—Theme and Variations from Suite No. 3 in G, Op. 55. Five Parts.   Mazeppa—Cossack Dance (Side 6)
C 3338—40

Exclusively on
"HIS MASTER'S VOICE"

THE GRAMOPHONE COMPANY LIMITED, HAYES, MIDDLESEX

Advertisement for the one of the Liverpool Philharmonic Orchestra's first recordings on HMV.

Autographs of William Walton, Henry Holst and Malcolm Sargent. Walton had conducted his own music earlier during the war, including the Liverpool première of his *Violin Concerto*.

The programme for the first concert given by the Liverpool Philharmonic Orchestra outside its home town. Appropriately, it was at Preston, where the orchestra still gives concerts today.

Programme featuring the conductor Rudolph Dunbar.

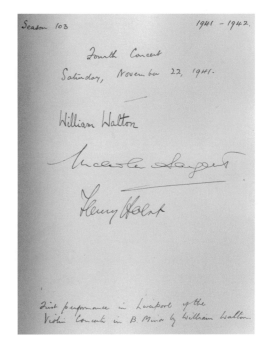

NEW VICTORIA CINEMA, PRESTON

The
Liverpool Philharmonic Orchestra

Leader	-	HENRY HOLST
Solo Pianoforte	-	MOISEIWITSCH
Conductors	-	HERBERT MENGES

SUNDAY, 21st DECEMBER, 1941
at 3 p.m.

Carnegie Trust Concert

Programme 3d.

PHILHARMONIC HALL, LIVERPOOL

Sunday, December 20th, 1942, at 2.30

CONCERT
in aid of the
COLONIAL COMFORTS FUND
President of the Council—MARSHAL OF THE ROYAL AIR FORCE
VISCOUNT TRENCHARD, G.C.B., G.C.V.O., D.S.O.

THE
Liverpool Philharmonic Orchestra

Soloist :
JOSEPH WEÏNGARTEN

Conductor :
RUDOLPH DUNBAR

Programme and Notes
SIXPENCE   Steinway Pianoforte

Sir Malcolm Sargent

Born: Ashford, Kent, 1895
Died: 1967
Principal Conductor: 1942-1948

Malcolm Sargent's father was a coal merchant, but in his spare time he was also a gifted amateur musician and church organist. His mother was the matron of a local school. By the age of sixteen, Malcolm was already an Associate of the Royal College of Organists and two years later he was awarded a music degree by Durham University. Sir Henry Wood gave him the opportunity to conduct at The Proms in 1921 and he was a regular fixture from then on, becoming one of the best known English conductors. He was a hard task master and served as Principal Conductor of the Hallé Orchestra from 1939 to 1942, moving to Liverpool for the following six years. He was knighted in 1947 and became Chief Conductor of The Proms from 1948 to 1967, and of the BBC Symphony Orchestra from 1950 to 1957. He was particularly highly regarded as a choral conductor. In his obituary, *The Times* said he 'was of all British conductors in his day most widely esteemed by the lay public ... a fluent, attractive pianist, a brilliant score-reader, a skilful and effective arranger and orchestrator.'

The Liverpool Philharmonic Orchestra with its Principal Conductor Malcolm Sargent, 1945.

Orchestra List 1943-44 season. For the first time in the Philharmonic's history, there were women players in the orchestra.

Season 1943—1944

THE

Liverpool Philharmonic Orchestra

Leader—HENRY HOLST

Principal Conductor :
DR. MALCOLM SARGENT

First Violins :

Henry Holst
Horace Cropper
Percy Ainley
Miss Edith Allanby
Edward Bennett
George Baker
Frederick Hanley
Maurice Kruger
Miss Cecilia Ormerod
George Roche
Julian Shelley
John Whitehead
William Chapman

Second Violins :
David Wise
Arthur Rowland
Clement de Mont
John Bailey
Frank Creswell
Miss Edith Horsfall
Miss Dorothy Lofthouse
James Maddocks
Miss Thelma Maden
Miss Mabel Whipp

Violas :
Herbert Downes
Lawrence Lackland
George Clarkson
Eugene Genin
George Mason
Bertram Srawley
Miss Isabel Mc Cullagh
Frank Starkey

Violoncellos :
Anthony Pini
Leonard Collinson
Edgar Coppin
Reginald Dovey
Horace Knussen
Miss Mary McCullagh
Sidney Lunt
Frank Sutton

Double Basses :
George Antoney
Willy Allan
William Sawyer
Robert Brown
Frank Sturman
David Thomson

Flutes :
Arthur Ackroyd
Miss Carrie Millars
Jack Maine

Piccolo :
Jack Maine

Oboes :
John McCarthy
Thomas Brearley

Cor Anglais :
Thomas Brearley

Clarinets :
Reginald Kell
Percy Hatton
Leonard Bryant

Bass Clarinet :
Leonard Bryant

Bassoons :
John Alexandra
Albert Entwistle

Horns :
John Johnson
William Waller
Edmund Chapman
Paul Engel

Trumpets :
Handel Hone
John Spencer
Harry Preston

Trombones :
Frederick Devlin
Frederick Launn
Robert Ball

Tuba :
Alec. Mortimer

Tympani :
John Casson

Percussion :
Harold Ball
John Welch

Harp :
Miss Rae Russell

W. R. FELL, *Secretary,*
The Liverpool Philharmonic Society Ltd.

Sargent's arrival at the Phil coincided with a spectacular explosion in the amount of music-making by the orchestra. In the 1942-1943 season, the orchestra played 124 full concerts and 15 children's concerts, and took part in no fewer than 16 recording sessions. Sixty-seven of the concerts were in Liverpool and Sargent conducted a total of 66 concerts inside and outside the City. Just a year later, the Liverpool Phil itself promoted 191 concerts with a further 13 children's concerts. All of the latter were conducted by Malcolm Sargent and he also wielded the baton at 127 other concerts. 109 concerts were given in Liverpool itself. Triumphantly, the Committee noted that the audiences for the Society's concerts had grown from 10,359 in the 1938-1939 season to 127,369 in the 1943-44 season.

The latter figure included 22,000 school children and Sargent made a point of connecting with the younger generation, as shown by this report in the *Evening Express* on 11th February 1944:

> Dr Malcolm Sargent conducted the Liverpool Philharmonic orchestra this afternoon at the third concert for Liverpool Elementary schoolchildren.
>
> The concert was organised by Liverpool Philharmonic Society in conjunction with the Liverpool Education Committee.
>
> Dr Sargent began by asking all those children present who had never seen him before to put up their hands. The majority of the children present did so.
>
> 'You ought to be ashamed of yourselves', he said.
>
> He then asked all the children who had never been in the Philharmonic Hall before to raise their hands. Again the majority responded.
>
> 'This is awful', said Dr Sargent.
>
> Introducing the children to the members of the orchestra, Dr Sargent said, 'This orchestra is one of the most famous in the country. It is Liverpool's orchestra. It is yours'.

Dr Sargent gave the children racy comments on the items of the programme, which included Beethoven's Overture *Leonore No. 3*, Handel's *Royal Firework Music* and the third and fourth movements from Tchaikovsky's *Fourth Symphony*.

It is hard for us today to understand just how difficult it must have been to keep the Phil running smoothly in wartime Britain. In a speech given in 1945, after the fighting was over, W.R. Fell, the Society's Secretary, told how he was proud of the fact that despite war-time travelling difficulties which beset the orchestra, the Phil's players never missed a concert, never cancelled one and never began one late.

The Foreword to the Syllabus for the 1941-42 season touches on the Phil's wartime challenges:

> It is not always easy to find players particularly for certain sections of the orchestra. Difficulties of transport both local and national make trying conditions for players and conductors. It is even impossible to be certain of the arrival of scores. But above all, it is difficult for promoters to be sure of audiences … A musician's skill is the result of years of work and the playing of symphonic music needs much practice. It is important that such skill should not be allowed to fall into disuse. These wartime concerts will go far to ensuring the music of peace.

Later in the season, even the interval tea break was withdrawn:

> The Committee regret to announce that owing to wartime difficulties of staff and supplies, refreshments will not be available at these concerts until further notice. At today's concert and in the future the interval will last only ten minutes.

The orchestra made its first appearance in London in 1944, at the Royal Albert Hall. The programme included Haydn's *Symphony No. 13*, Smetana's *From Bohemia's Woods and Fields* and Dvořák's *Symphony No. 3*. The soloist for the

Season 105   1943/4

Fifteenth Concert
March 18th, 1944.

Basil Cameron

Clifford Curzon

Benjamin Britten

Season 105   Sixteenth Concert   1943/4
March 26th, 1944

Victor Harding   Malcolm Sargent

Edward Reach.

Kathleen Ferrier

PHILHARMONIC HALL   MONDAY AFTERNOON
Liverpool   November 27th 1944 at 2-30

SEASON 1944—1945

SECOND CONCERT
FOR
SECONDARY SCHOOLS

Dr. MALCOLM SARGENT

conducts the

Liverpool Philharmonic Orchestra

Leader : DAVID WISE

PROGRAMME

Overture "Ruy Blas"	Mendelssohn	(1809-1847)
Suite from the Dramatic Music	...Purcell	(1658-1695)
A Children's Overture	Quilter	(1877)
"Carillon" for Orator and Orchestra ...	... Elgar	(1857-1937)
Orator : FRANK PHILLIPS		
Marche Militaire	Schubert	(1797-1828)

Dr. Malcolm Sargent will give brief verbal
comments on the music to be performed

This Concert has been organised by The Liverpool Philharmonic
Society Ltd., in conjunction with the Liverpool Education Committee

P.T.O.

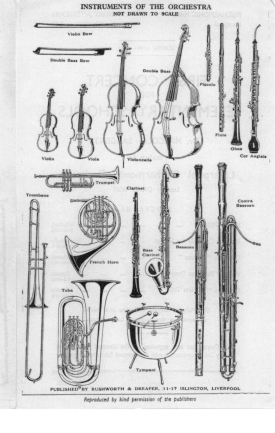

INSTRUMENTS OF THE ORCHESTRA
NOT DRAWN TO SCALE

Violin Bow

Double Bass Bow

Double Bass

Piccolo

Flute

Violin   Viola   Violoncella   Oboe   Cor Anglais

Trombone   Trumpet   Clarinet   Contra Bassoon

French Horn   Bass Clarinet   Bassoon

Tuba

Tympani

PUBLISHED BY RUSHWORTH & DREAPER, 11-17 ISLINGTON, LIVERPOOL

Reproduced by kind permission of the publishers

A CONCERT of RUSSIAN MUSIC

to commemorate the

23rd ANNIVERSARY

of the

RED ARMY

Liverpool
Philharmonic Orchestra

Leader : HENRY HOLST

Conductor : LOUIS COHEN

Soloist : NOEL MEWTON-WOOD

*PROGRAMME
FOURPENCE*

—

PHILHARMONIC HALL

SUNDAY, 21st FEBRUARY, 1943, at 2-30

The presence of His Majesty's Forces at these Sunday Concerts is made
possible by co-operation with the Lord Mayor of Liverpool's War Fund.
Donations to this fund will be gladly received by the Hon. Treasurer,
J. M. Furniss, Martins Bank, Water Street, Liverpool.

THE CITY OF LIVERPOOL VICTORY CONCERT

LIVERPOOL PHILHARMONIC ORCHESTRA

CONDUCTED BY

Sir THOMAS BEECHAM *Bart.*

♪ V ♪ V ♪

LIVERPOOL PHILHARMONIC HALL
FRIDAY SEPTEMBER 28th AT 6·30 p.m.

Liverpool Philharmonic Orchestra

EIGHT CONCERTS FOR THE

MAN IN THE STREET

Conductor :
Dr.
MALCOLM
SARGENT

JULY 5th to JULY 12th 1947

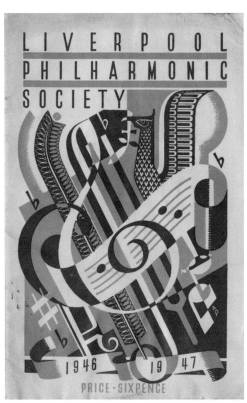

LIVERPOOL PHILHARMONIC SOCIETY

1946 19 47

PRICE · SIXPENCE

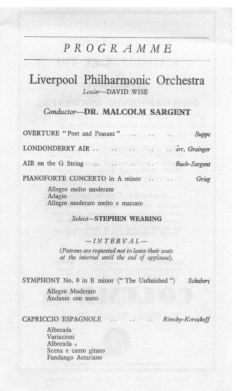

PROGRAMME

Liverpool Philharmonic Orchestra

*Leader—*DAVID WISE

Conductor—DR. MALCOLM SARGENT

OVERTURE " Poet and Peasant " .. .. ..   *Suppe*

LONDONDERRY AIR .. ..   *arr. Grainger*

AIR on the G String .. ..   *Bach-Sargent*

PIANOFORTE CONCERTO in A minor .. ..   *Grieg*

    Allegro molto moderato
    Adagio
    Allegro moderato molto e marcato

    Soloist—**STEPHEN WEARING**

—INTERVAL—

(Patrons are requested not to leave their seats
at the interval until the end of applause).

SYMPHONY No. 8 in B minor (" The Unfinished ")   *Schubert*

    Allegro Moderato
    Andante con moto

CAPRICCIO ESPAGNOLE .. .. ..   *Rimsky-Korsakoff*

    Alborada
    Variazioni
    Alborada
    Scena e canto gitano
    Fandango Asturiano

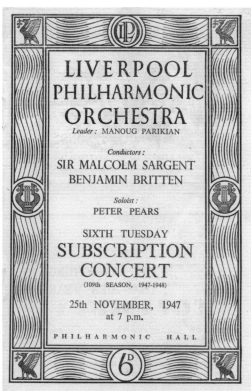

LIVERPOOL PHILHARMONIC ORCHESTRA

Leader : MANOUG PARIKIAN

Conductors :

SIR MALCOLM SARGENT
BENJAMIN BRITTEN

Soloist :
PETER PEARS

SIXTH TUESDAY
SUBSCRIPTION
CONCERT

(109th SEASON, 1947-1948)

25th NOVEMBER, 1947
at 7 p.m.

PHILHARMONIC HALL

6D

Delius *Violin Concerto* was Albert Sammons and the conductor was the redoubtable Malcolm Sargent.

Classical music was seen as being beneficial to the wider war effort and it was no longer the preserve of a rich elite. Instead, the Philharmonic Hall's doors were flung open to all comers. The Society boasted that the admission prices for its Sunday afternoon concerts were 'lower for the general public than for any comparable series in the country'.

In a further attempt to widen the appeal of the Phil, the orchestra began a series of 'The Man in the Street' concerts. These proved to be an incredibly popular innovation and existed as part of an initiative called 'Holidays at Home'. In 1944, the *Evening Express* reported:

> The audience attending these concerts are generally very youthful: girls in their late teens or early twenties, and men and women in the Services, including many from USA.

> 'Audiences today', Dr Malcolm Sargent, conductor of the orchestra, told me, 'do not attend the concerts for amusement. They come for recreation, in the true sense of being recreated from a tired spirit'.

> Symphonies, he said, are great favourites with Liverpool audiences. Works by Tchaikovsky, Dvořák and Wagner receive tremendous applause.

> 'I am proud of this orchestra', Dr Sargent stated. 'We are giving 15 concerts, each in a varied style, and the orchestra has given first class standard performances each day'.

> Dr Sargent believes the popular type of concert does have a strong educational value. No cheap music is played. The only thing about the concerts which is cheap, he said, is the price of admission.

> Dr Sargent maintains that just as welfare work will be one of the most important sections in post-war business, music will be equally important in leisure.

Programme for a Concert celebrating the 23rd anniversary of the Red Army.

Concert programme commemorating Victory in the War.

Cover of the 'Man In The Street' Concerts Programme.

Syllabus for the 1946-1947 season.

The programme of the very first Industrial Concert at Philharmonic Hall.

Programme for a concert featuring Benjamin Britten and Peter Pears.

These 'Man in the Street' Concerts continued on after the end of the war, but were eventually dropped. A new series of industrial concerts was launched in 1946. This new idea attracted attention – and considerable amounts of praise – from all over the country.

The Institute of Directors profiled the Liverpool Philharmonic's work in a publication called 'Investing in the Arts':

> The Liverpool Philharmonic called a meeting, on a directorate level, of representatives from about twenty of the large Merseyside firms. They proposed to put on an experimental concert at the lowest possible price (at that time 3/6) for any seat in the house. The twenty firms were not asked to subsidize the event, but merely to appoint someone to publicise the concert in the works, to collect the seat prices and distribute the tickets. The pioneer concert of this scheme, conducted by Sir Malcolm Sargent, was an instantaneous success, and three similar concerts were laid on during that particular season. So popular did they become that a rationing system had to be adopted for the participating firms. Moreover, each ration contained a proportion of seats in each part of the concert hall. If a firm's allocation was 100 seats in all, 35 would be stalls, 20 the upper stalls, 30 in the balcony, 10 on the platform and 5 in a box. Most firms used to ballot for tickets (all priced equally at 3/6) and a pleasant piquancy was added to the scheme by the fact that an office boy might get a place in the box while the managing director enjoyed the experience of a seat in the balcony. This element of the luck of the draw was an interesting psychological angle to the plan.

> The name Industrial Concerts may not be an ideal one, but the plan certainly is. Everyone involved derives benefit from it. The Royal Liverpool Philharmonic Orchestra secures a stable and substantial revenue from 24 block-booked concerts each season. The firms appreciate the amenity which the concerts provide for their workers,

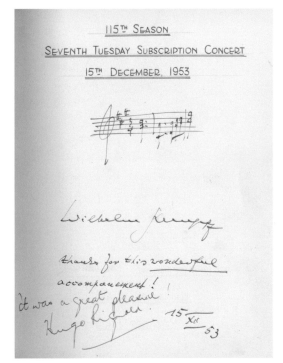

and the audiences are assured of inexpensive and enjoyable entertainment. It is also a fact that many of those who visit these concerts had never been to an orchestral concert before in their lives, and that large numbers of them have graduated to more advanced musical programmes.

Those who may wonder how such cut-price programmes are possible will appreciate the principal reason: the publicity costs are much reduced because the only printing involved is the advance leaflet. No costly posters are necessary, and no press-advertising. One way and another these Industrial Concerts are a sound and rewarding venture. They deserve to be developed in many other cities.

In October 1946, Sargent conducted the Liverpool Philharmonic in the première of Benjamin Britten's *The Young Person's Guide to the Orchestra*, with the man who wrote the accompanying words, Eric Crozier, providing the narration. The Phil's recording of the work received the award for the best orchestral record of the year at the Annual Conference of Music and Gramophone Critics in New York two years later.

Once the war was over, some of those players who had moved to Liverpool to escape The Blitz returned to London. In February 1948, Sir Malcolm Sargent gave an interview to the *Daily Post* correspondent, W.F. Stewart. He was asked to comment on the feeling in some quarters that there had been a falling off in the quality of playing at recent concerts. His reply was emphatic:

'That sort of talk makes me very angry', Sir Malcolm declared. For a man of such amazing fluency, he almost spluttered in his indignation.

'When we lost some of our star players many people, I agree, thought the orchestra would go down hill. Well, they were wrong. It is now a better entity – it has a better ensemble – than ever. The orchestra plays a great deal better than it often gets credit for.

Gramophone records, of course, are the real test of an orchestra. You simply cannot play badly and get away with it on records. Don't forget that all records that are made are not published; some don't come up to standard when they are played on the gramophone company's test turntables; they are therefore scrapped. That has never happened to Liverpool's fine orchestra.

To sum up, the orchestra is doing very fine work – some of the works in our repertoire simply couldn't be done better.'

Sir Malcolm mentioned that during his foreign tours it was tremendously encouraging to see people actually playing the orchestra's recordings and enthusing over the quality of the performances.

Incidentally, the Liverpool-made records are earning dollars for Britain. Three-quarters of a million recordings of *Messiah* alone were sold within a few months in the United States.

The Berlin Philharmonic Orchestra performed at the Philharmonic Hall in November 1948. It was their second visit under their conductor, Wilhelm Furtwängler. Their welcome was just as warm as it had been in 1928 and it was hoped that this sort of cultural exchange would help to heal some of the post-war wounds between Britain and Germany.

Sir Malcolm Sargent resigned as Principal Conductor at the end of the 1947-1948 season, but remained as Principal Guest Conductor for a further year. He had presided over the busiest period in the Liverpool Philharmonic's history to date. His time in charge had seen radical changes for the better on the platform and a new desire to engage with all areas of the community, which has remained at the heart of the Phil's activities ever since.

Hugo Rignold

Born: Kingston-upon-Thames, 1905
Died: 1976
Principal Conductor: 1948–1954

Hugo Rignold's background could not have been more musical: his father was a conductor and his mother, an opera singer. He studied at the Royal Academy of Music and played violin in a string of jazz groups and dance bands, including Mantovani's orchestra. While serving with the RAF, he conducted the Palestine Orchestra (now the Israel Philharmonic). After spending a year as a Staff Conductor at the Royal Opera House, he joined the Liverpool Philharmonic as Principal Conductor in 1948. After leaving the Phil in 1954, he went on to be Music Director of the Royal Ballet between 1957 and 1960 and to be Principal Conductor of the City of Birmingham Symphony Orchestra from 1960 to 1968. He earned well in his dance band days and was able to afford a racing car, which he often drove at the famous Brooklands track.

Hugo Rignold did not have the easiest of rides during his time in Liverpool. To some, his background as a jazz and dance band player made his classical credentials deeply suspect and he was given a frosty welcome by a section of the Phil's supporters. Just six months after being handed the Conductor's job, he resigned, giving an interview to the *News Review*, headlined 'The Bigots of Liverpool':

> 'I couldn't stand it any more', said Hugo Rignold. 'I had hoped to be happy in Liverpool. I knew I could make good with the orchestra. I have done. But thanks to a bigoted and musically-snobbish few, my stay here has been anything but pleasant ...' The orchestra will be sorry to see him go. 'He is a first class man', said one of the players last week. 'Even though he was a strong disciplinarian, there was not a man or woman in the orchestra who would not do anything for him ...' Rignold explained his resentment. Certain Philharmonic patrons, he disclosed, had written to him and to the local Press accusing him of 'dragging the orchestra down to dance-band levels ...' Wilfred Stiff, 30-year-old manager of the Philharmonic Society, thinks Rignold's season has been 'the most successful in the orchestra's history'. He agrees with Rignold in blaming 'a few bigoted and hot-headed people who worship big names and who have made his life a misery in almost a criminal fashion'.

Just a month later, Rignold seemed to be more certain of his future with the Liverpool Phil, when he signed a new contract with the Society, which gave him responsibility for the artistic direction of the orchestra. He promptly announced that he would not be renewing the contracts of twenty-two of the players.

Rignold told the *Liverpool Echo*:

> It is not a question of dismissal or sack. Members of the orchestra are on a one year's contract, and whether that contract is renewed or not depends on whether I feel they are up to the standard I consider necessary. All I am concerned with is improving the standard of playing. I have in mind several ideas for the orchestra, and one of them concerns the 1951 festival [the Festival of Britain]. By that time I hope to get the very best possible players obtainable for our orchestra and I won't rest until I do so.

The Musicians' Union took up the sacked players' cause and arguments over the case raged in the local press. In June, a month after the proposal had been made public, the Society's Chairman and Executive Committee resigned en masse, to be replaced by an interim Committee. Three months later, the dispute was settled. Under the new deal, all players in the orchestra were given a contract for nine months to take them through until the end of the 1949-1950 season, subject to three months' notice on either side. After that, the players were offered continuous contracts, also subject to three months' notice of termination. The *Evening Express* reported the Society's Chairman, Alderman Luke Hogan, as saying that Hugo Rignold was 'happy to co-operate with all concerned in making the new contract scheme work satisfactorily in the interests of the Society'.

In 1950, the Committee decided in secret to replace Rignold with Enrique Jorda, but a member of the Committee informed the press and started a campaign to keep Rignold, with the result that the Arts Council and Liverpool City Council threatened to withdraw support. Unfortunately, the Committee neglected to tell Jorda, who arrived in Britain to conclude negotiations, only to find out that Rignold had been retained.

The music-making carried on at the Phil, with the soap opera over who was to conduct the orchestra continuing to play out in the background. As ever, Handel's *Messiah* was performed to enthusiastic audiences in December 1950. But there were rumblings of discontent from the ranks of the singers. The choir secretary wrote to the Society's chairman to say:

> These numerous renderings of *Messiah* – four each Christmas – receive our enthusiastic support out of sheer loyalty to the Society; the vast majority of our members would be pleased to let the work rest for ten years.

In 1953, there was more controversy in the local press – this time over an application for a licence to sell 'intoxicants' at the Philharmonic Hall. Up until that point, concertgoers had only been able to buy soft drinks. The members of the Liverpool Temperance Cabinet were outraged. The counsel for the Society successfully argued that 'Coach parties travelling from up to 100 miles away from the City often required something more stimulating than tea or coffee, particularly in bad weather. At the interval of a concert many people visited public houses nearby. When, on their return, the performance had recommenced, some disturbance was inevitable and inconvenient.'

In a letter to the *Evening Express*, a member of the Liverpool Temperance Cabinet outlined their objections:

Another way the Liverpool Philharmonic widened its audience was through its Promenade Concerts at Liverpool Stadium. This was from a concert in July 1955, with Hugo Rignold conducting and Benno Moiseiwitsch at the piano.

Syllabus for the 1955–1956 season, which was successful despite the absence of Paul Kletzki.

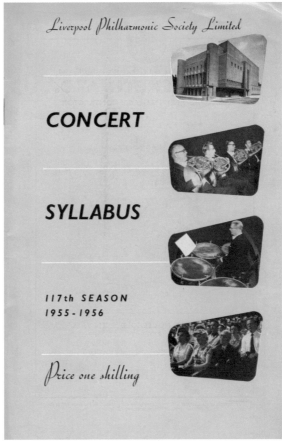

Liverpool Philharmonic Society Limited

CONCERT

SYLLABUS

117th SEASON
1955 - 1956

Price one shilling

How foolish to spend £4,000 to meet the wishes of a few clients who need stimulants when their brethren, who frequent the less cultural entertainment of football, are obliged week by week to go outside the Everton and Liverpool grounds for their refreshment at half-time! We understand there is no first-class football club in the country (except the Arsenal, which has a bar facing outside the ground) which has a licence for the sale of intoxicating drink … What a pity the Philharmonic Hall cannot be left as it is – a place of culture and refinement, where our young people can enjoy a chat with their friends during the interval over nothing more harmful than a cup of coffee. No one's pleasure would be reduced thereby, and no one need have any worry over possible consequences!

The fact that the Society's Executive Committee had been prepared to apply for a drinks licence in the first place suggests that the organisation was now being run by a more enlightened and forward-looking group of individuals. The new Chairman of the Society, Alderman D.J. Lewis, was keen to reach out to new audiences. He told the *Liverpool Echo* in September 1954:

So far as I am concerned, and speaking for myself, so long as every seat is occupied and the people have paid for their tickets they can come here in their overalls if they wish … If people, including myself, are fortunate enough to have an old dinner jacket or an old claw-hammered coat and a laundered white waistcoat in which they wish to come, then I would welcome them all. But this is a democratic institution, and at no time am I going to say to an annual general meeting of members that I wish you to go back to the stiff shirts at all. No! It can come along naturally if it wishes to, but so far as I personally am concerned, I am quite comfortable for the young people and any others to come along on a Tuesday evening – and for that matter on any evening – and occupy the stalls when the orchestra is performing. That is the sole object and intent of this very practical committee, and long may it reign.

Surprising as it may seem, given his relationship with parts of the orchestra and the Society, by the time he left the Phil in 1954, Hugo Rignold was actually regarded with a good deal of respect and he regularly returned to the City as a guest conductor. His time with the Liverpool Philharmonic had heightened his credentials as a leading classical conductor and he went on to work successfully with the Royal Ballet and the City of Birmingham Symphony Orchestra.

The Polish conductor and composer Paul Kletzki was lined up as a replacement for Rignold in the 1954-1955 season, along with the Englishman John Pritchard. However, at the very last minute Kletzki pulled out, citing issues over his work permit. The Society had been badly let down; Pritchard carried on alone. He was joined by Efrem Kurtz as joint Principal Conductor in the 1955-1956 and 1956-1957 seasons.

Efrem Kurtz

Born: St Petersburg, 1900
Died: 1995
Principal Conductor 1955–1957

Efrem Kurtz studied at the St Petersburg Conservatoire, with the composer Alexander Glazunov numbering among his teachers. His conducting engagements before he joined the Liverpool Philharmonic included the Berlin Philharmonic, the Stuttgart Philharmonic, the Ballet Russe de Monte Carlo, the Kansas City Philharmonic and the Houston Symphony Orchestra. He was one of the early stars of the classical gramophone industry, usually recording either with the Philharmonia Orchestra or with the New York Philharmonic. He was awarded a gold disc for 3 million record sales in 1953. He returned to Russia in 1966 for a period, conducting orchestras in Leningrad and Moscow.

Efrem Kurtz decided to leave the Phil and return to life as a freelance conductor in 1957, leaving John Pritchard as the sole Principal Conductor through until 1963.

Chapter Six

By Royal Command

Neil Hitt, Principal Timpani and Josephine Large,
Percussion, Royal Liverpool Philharmonic Orchestra.
Photographed at Abercromby Square, Liverpool.

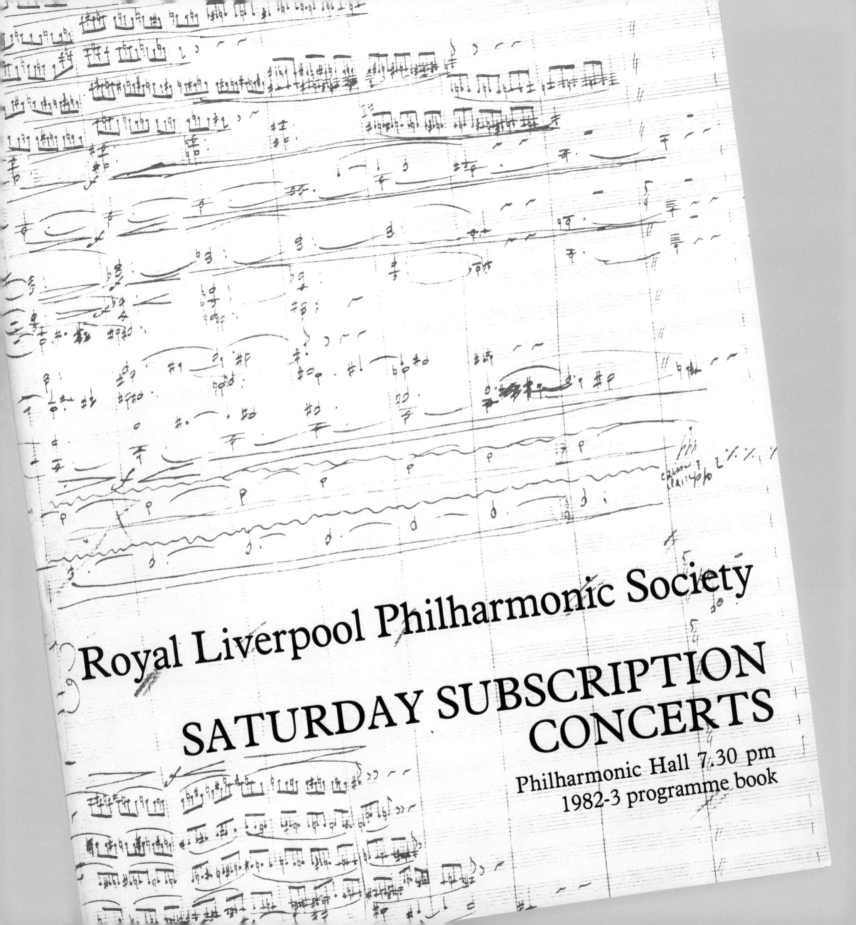

Royal Liverpool Philharmonic Society

SATURDAY SUBSCRIPTION CONCERTS

Philharmonic Hall 7.30 pm
1982-3 programme book

Royal Approval

In 1957, the *London Gazette* announced that the Liverpool Philharmonic Society and Orchestra was to be granted 'Royal' status. From that moment on, the organisation that we know today as the Liverpool Phil came into existence. At the time, the Phil was the first orchestra outside of London to be granted the honour of being allowed to use the word 'Royal' in its title. A year later, Her Majesty the Queen became the Orchestra's Patron – a role she has retained ever since.

Sir John Pritchard

Born: London, 1921
Died: 1989
Principal Conductor: 1955-1963

John Pritchard's father was a violinist in the London Symphony Orchestra. He studied violin, piano and conducting in Italy. A conscientious objector, he refused to serve in the forces during the Second World War, although he was medically unfit to do so anyway. His conducting career began with the semi-professional Derby String Orchestra, from where he moved to Glyndebourne in 1947, becoming chorus master in 1949. He was with the Royal Liverpool Philharmonic from 1955 to 1963, jointly with Efrem Kurtz for the first two years and then on his own for the next six. In 1963, he returned to Glyndebourne as conductor, becoming Principal Conductor from 1968 and then Music Director from 1969 to 1978. He also regularly conducted the Royal Philharmonic Orchestra and the Vienna Symphony Orchestra and at the Royal Opera House and Vienna State Opera. Later in his life, he was music director of the London Philharmonic Orchestra, chief conductor of the BBC Symphony Orchestra and music director of Cologne Opera and San Francisco Opera. He was knighted in 1983.

Young Conductors' Competition

In 1958, the Royal Liverpool Philharmonic Society began a series of international competitions for conductors, under a judging panel led by John Pritchard and William Steinberg, the conductor of the Pittsburgh Symphony Orchestra. One of the first three joint winners was the young Indian conductor, Zubin Mehta, who was appointed the RLPO's associate conductor for a year as his prize. He went on to hold permanent positions with many of the world's leading orchestras, including the Montreal Symphony Orchestra, the Los Angeles Philharmonic Orchestra, the Israel Philharmonic Orchestra and the Bavarian State Opera. He probably achieved his biggest international audience as the conductor of the *Three Tenors* first concert in Rome in 1990.

These conducting competitions were replaced in 1968 by a series of seminars, which gave young British conductors the chance to work with a professional orchestra. Beneficiaries of this series included Andrew Davis and John Eliot Gardiner, both of whom went on to be among the finest British conductors of their generation.

Musica Viva

At the time of his appointment, Pritchard was the youngest conductor in the Phil's history. His time in charge marked a particularly innovative period for the orchestra, not least in his championing of contemporary music. The RLPO's world première recording of Michael Tippett's oratorio *A Child of Our Time* was given wide acclaim by the critics. *The Times* said:

> It could scarcely be better performed than in John Pritchard's conducting of the Liverpool Philharmonic Chorus and Orchestra ... the recording is colourful and amazingly realistic.

Record News gave the Royal Liverpool Philharmonic Choir 'top marks' and said:

> John Pritchard's sensitive direction of both works ... reveals all the details with careful skill. Soloists and orchestra are excellent throughout. The recording must have been a difficult job, but succeeds in bringing

everything clearly to the ear, being especially successful in the spirituals where the combinations of soloists, choir and orchestra can only sound right or wrong, there being no middle course.

While, in *Gramophone Record Review*, the orchestra was described as being in 'wonderful form':

> Indeed, it invites comparison with any of the London Orchestras in this performance which pays tribute to the splendid training of John Pritchard.

The last word on the subject goes to *The Gramophone*, which particularly praised the recording, but also said:

> The performance is, almost without qualification, a superb one.

Pritchard was a man with a mission when it came to converting Liverpool audiences to contemporary classical music. He launched a series of concerts called 'Musica Viva', which showcased new works. Its success caught the imagination of the classical music press and was given huge national coverage. Copycat Musica Viva seasons quickly sprang up around the country in venues as far apart as Edinburgh and London. In an interview with *The Times* in January 1959, Pritchard explained that his pioneering series in Liverpool had been far more successful than he had originally expected:

> The major orchestral repertory forms the substance of the regular subscription concerts, but it is my own personal interest to introduce modern works lasting for 20 to 25 minutes into the subscription concerts and not affect the box office, although I know that contemporary music has an adverse effect on audiences in other cities – in London for example. But one programme we played in Liverpool to a capacity audience consisted of Mozart's 39th Symphony, Stravinsky's *Symphony in Three Movements* and the *Emperor Concerto*, played by Andor Foldes; another contained Matyas Seiber's cantata *Ulysses* and Tchaikovsky's first Piano Concerto, with Shura Cherkassky as soloist. The public accepts this formula and has sufficient interest to say 'I will give this new work a trial because at the same time I

The Royal Liverpool Philharmonic Orchestra with its Principal Conductor, John Pritchard.

Zubin Mehta, one of the winners of the First International Conductors' Competition, 1958.

Programme for the final of the first International Conductors' Competition in Liverpool, 1958.

ROYAL LIVERPOOL PHILHARMONIC SOCIETY

PATRON - HER MAJESTY THE QUEEN

INTERNATIONAL
CONDUCTORS' COMPETITION

DIRECTORS

WILLIAM STEINBERG   JOHN PRITCHARD

FINAL PUBLIC
PERFORMANCES

BY

COMPETITORS

Wednesday 21 and Thursday 22 May 1958 at 7-30 p.m.

PROGRAMME
Thursday 22 May

PRICE SIXPENCE

The Grand Foyer Bar,
Philharmonic Hall, 1950s.

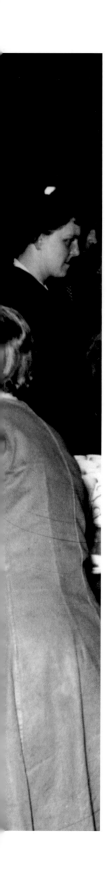

can hear a marvellous performance of one of my favourites'. Our audiences are openly critical and express their opinions by applause, but they will show an interest in modern music.

Musica Viva grew from the need to expand the repertory. The management willingly agreed to run the first series almost regardless of box-office returns; a ticket for the entire series costs five shillings. Our intention was to give Liverpool an opportunity to hear contemporary works, to gain kudos and to stimulate the orchestra. We expected an audience of perhaps 120, but on most occasions now we can expect that figure to be quadrupled.

The *Daily Express* critic, Noel Goodwin, reported back favourably from a trip to Liverpool:

For some time Liverpool has been ahead of other orchestral cities in Britain in giving audiences the chance to be musically up to date. It has done so with a series of arresting, provocative concerts called 'Musica Viva', each featuring typical works by composers of the present day. Even with the fresher breeze that has lately begun to penetrate the murk of London's convention-choked concert life, a programme such as I heard in Liverpool's Philharmonic Hall last night would still be quite remote there.

The Phil's performance of Alban Berg's symphonic suite *Lulu* in one Musica Viva concert in 1959 was covered by *Woman* magazine – not the most likely place to find a review of a cutting edge contemporary concert. The article was headlined 'SHE SCREAMED – for 10s. 6d. A second!' and it told how an actress was required to stand off stage and scream at the end of *Lulu*, as directed by John Pritchard:

Hilary Crane stood in the wings of the theatre. 'No, no, no', she shrilled. Then she screamed. The scream rose to a blood-chilling shriek and ended with a low-pitched gurgle.

'Quite the quickest part I've ever played … It lasted four seconds, and at a fee of two guineas that's not a bad rate of pay.'

Twenty-four year old Hilary is an actress. Her scream, the best and most fearsome she has ever produced, brought to an end the Royal Liverpool Philharmonic Orchestra's production of *Lulu*.

Unseen by the audience, Hilary was pretending to be Lulu, stabbed by Jack the Ripper. She had to give the scream the realism it needed.

'I hope I succeeded. I know I nearly convinced myself. I could almost feel the prick of the murderer's knife!'

There has always been a respectful rivalry between the Royal Liverpool Philharmonic and the Hallé Orchestra, not least over which is the senior of the two orchestras. In 1959, the Phil achieved a notable coup with the announcement that it would be replacing the Manchester band in performing a week of concerts at the Royal Albert Hall in London, under the baton of John Pritchard.

Pritchard took the opportunity to take some of his Musica Viva thinking to the London audience and the concerts included Stravinsky's *Symphony in Three Movements;* Webern's *Six Pieces, Op. 6;* Schoenberg's *Variations, Op. 31;* and a piece which is now a concert favourite, but at the time was described as a 'rarity': Richard Strauss's *Also Sprach Zarathustra.* The visit to London passed with great acclaim, but it was not the only time in 1960 that the Phil went on the road.

The Royal Liverpool Philharmonic Society had commissioned Sir William Walton to compose a new symphony (his second) for Liverpool's Charter celebrations in 1955. It took him five years to complete it and the new work finally received its première at the Edinburgh Festival in 1960. The *Edinburgh Evening News* praised the standard of the orchestra's musicianship as 'thrilling' and the *Daily Herald* said 'John Pritchard and the Royal Liverpool Philharmonic Orchestra gave the new symphony a splendid send-off.'

The '£200 – Or It's Off!' Pianist

The Society hit the headlines again in 1960, when the Chairman decided to make a very public stand against foreign soloists who pulled out of concerts at the last minute. It followed an incident involving the Hungarian pianist, György Cziffra. He had been booked to appear for a fee of £250, but at the last minute his agent demanded an increase of £200, or else he would not be turning up in Liverpool.

The Society's Chairman, Alderman Harry Livermore, was outraged, telling the *Daily Mail:*

> Five times this season we have been let down by foreign artists. In each case the Society has so far protected the artist concerned. But in doing so we have come in for a great deal of criticism from the public. So the

John Pritchard and William Walton looking over the score of Walton's *Symphony No.2*, which Pritchard and the Royal Liverpool Philharmonic Orchestra premièred in 1960.

Musica Viva programme cover.

committee has decided now to tell the whole truth. Bookings for his concert, which was to have included the Tchaikovsky Concerto, of which he is a great exponent, have been excellent ... If this sort of thing should happen again, we may have to resort to legal action.

Both the Phil and the pianist refused to back down and he did not appear in concert.

Musical Apprenticeships

In 1961, Alderman Livermore was back in the national newspapers, this time on a happier subject: the announcement of a new scheme to give up to twenty young musicians studying at conservatoires 'part-time apprenticeships' with the Royal Liverpool Philharmonic. The programme, which was new to Britain, was created in an attempt to give the students experience of working with a professional symphony orchestra. Livermore told the *Daily Telegraph*:

In the nature of their training at academies and colleges of music, students concentrate on the technical study of their own instruments. They embark on their careers with a limited knowledge of the orchestral repertoire and even less idea of what life is like in a major orchestra. As a result, many potential orchestral players are lost.

The new scheme was greeted warmly by the Royal College of Music, the Royal Manchester College, the Guildhall School of Music and Trinity College.

The Swinging Sixties

By the early 1960s, there were other musicians in Liverpool who were gaining worldwide fame of their own. The City was a vibrant hotbed of pop music creativity, with names such as Billy Fury, Billy J. Kramer, Gerry and the Pacemakers, The Merseybeats, The Searchers and, of course, The Beatles topping the charts. In 1965, even local lad Ken Dodd spent five weeks at the top of the pop charts with *Tears*. That same year, the RLPO teamed up with the Liverpool band The Swinging Blue Jeans (of *Hippy Hippy Shake* fame) as part of a

The Royal Liverpool Philharmonic Orchestra with its newly appointed Principal Conductor, Charles Groves, 1963.

The massed ranks of the Royal Liverpool Philharmonic Orchestra and Choir for a performance of Mahler's 8th Symphony at Liverpool Cathedral.

concert of music of modern American composers. Alongside works by Leonard Bernstein, Samuel Barber and George Gershwin was a brand new piece especially commissioned by the RLPO from the young American composer, Carl Davis, which featured symphony orchestra and pop group. It was the beginning of a long relationship between the orchestra and Davis. He has been a regular visitor to the Philharmonic Hall ever since, specialising in 'Pops' concerts featuring crowd pleasing populist works, and becoming famous for the wide-ranging selection of jackets he wears on the rostrum. A columnist in the *Daily Post* said of his early foray into classical pop:

> It was thought that such a project might help to broaden the audience for serious music, introducing to the Phil people who might otherwise never go there. It might also, it occurs to me, introduce to beat music people who might otherwise never go to The Cavern.

It was not the first time that the Liverpool Phil had tipped its orchestral toe in the waters of crossover music. Five years earlier, in 1960, the RLPO put on a concert of 'serious works' for jazz orchestra and symphony orchestra, featuring Johnny Dankworth's orchestra. Alderman Livermore clearly saw attack as the best means of defence, when it came to explaining the concert to his more conservative subscribers. With a tone that did not invite further discussion on the subject, he told them:

> In case anybody raises eyebrows at this, I want to say that we regard it as an artistic exercise.

During this era, the Philharmonic Hall also started to play host to its first pop and jazz concerts. Artists included Buddy Holly, Sidney Bechet, Dizzy Gillespie and the Modern Jazz Quartet.

In 1963, John Pritchard ended his time as the RLPO's Principal Conductor, moving to Glyndebourne to concentrate on his growing operatic career. Considering that he had stepped in at the last minute following the Paul Kletzki affair in 1955, he had proven to be one of the most successful of the Phil's Principal Conductor appointments, taking the orchestra into artistic and geographical areas that would have been thought impossible only a couple of decades before.

The Phil's Committee was shrewd in the appointment of the new Principal Conductor, Charles Groves, a man who would prove to have the ability to continue to grow the orchestra's prestige following Pritchard's departure.

Sir Charles Groves

Born: London, 1915
Died: 1992
Principal Conductor: 1963–1977

Charles Groves studied at the Royal College of Music. He became an accompanist working for the BBC, before taking up the baton of the BBC Revue Orchestra in 1943. The following year he moved to conduct the BBC Northern Orchestra, where he stayed until 1951. Then he became Principal Conductor of the Bournemouth Symphony Orchestra, before taking over as Music Director of Welsh National Opera in 1961. He moved to Liverpool in 1963 and stayed for fourteen years. From 1967 until his death, he was Associate Conductor of the Royal Philharmonic Orchestra and in the 1970s, he became a regular conductor of the Last Night of the Proms. From 1978 to 1979, he was Music Director of English National Opera. He was knighted in 1973.

Charles Groves turned the Royal Liverpool Philharmonic into the most respected British orchestra outside London. During his time with the Phil, he said he conducted 'everything from the *St John Passion* to Messiaen and Stockhausen'. Spending as much as nine months a year with the orchestra meant that his relationship with the players and with the City was both deep and meaningful.

Groves made his name as a highly skilled conductor of large scale works. During his time with the RLPO, he was the first English conductor to direct a complete cycle of Mahler symphonies. When the RLPO performed Mahler's *Symphony No. 8* at The Proms in 1964, the Royal Albert Hall audience gave the orchestra a fifteen minute standing ovation. It was only the third time that the work had been performed in Britain.

Groves continued John Pritchard's work in encouraging modern composers and frequently programmed their pieces in the Phil's concerts. Respected both as a conductor of operatic and orchestral repertoire, Groves gained a reputation for excellence across the whole spectrum of classical music, rather than in one specific genre. Using a medical analogy, he said: 'I feel myself a GP rather than a consultant'. If there was one area in which he was regarded as being a particular expert, it was as an exponent of British music. He was a major champion of Delius, Vaughan Williams, Sullivan, Elgar and Walton.

In 1964, Edmund Tracey wrote an article in *The Observer* headlined 'Guiding lights on the Mersey'. It credited some of the success of the Royal Liverpool Philharmonic to the fact that the orchestra had its own hall in which to perform:

> After a month spent visiting some of our chief provincial music centres, I am coming to the conclusion that the most grievous single burden that English orchestras have to bear – greater even than their financial hardships – is their homelessness. The peripatetic miseries of London orchestral players are well known; but anyone who supposes that provincial bands are all comfortably established on their own premises is mistaken … There is only one orchestra in the country that regularly rehearses and plays in its own hall and that is the Royal Liverpool Philharmonic. And there is no doubt that this is one of the main reasons for its thriving success.

Peter Pears, Charles Groves, Heather Harper, Benjamin Britten and Thomas Hemsley in the Green Room at the Philharmonic in 1963, for the Liverpool première of Britten's *War Requiem*.

Celebrity Concert of 1967, which featured the great Italian baritone Tito Gobbi.

The conductor and composer Carl Davis has enjoyed a long relationship with the Phil which continues to this day.

Olivier Messiaen was in the Hall to hear the RLPO play his *Turangalîla Symphony* in 1968. He wrote: 'To mark the magnificent concert of 12th May … with my greatest joy and gratitude'.

Signature of the legendary classical guitarist, Andrés Segovia, on his visit to Liverpool in 1963.

Autograph of the great Spanish soprano, Victoria de los Angeles, on one of her many visits to Philharmonic Hall.

The great Russian cellist and conductor Mstislav Rostropovich signing the autograph book on his Liverpool debut in 1968.

On Tour

In 1966, the Phil gave its first overseas tour to Germany and Switzerland. It was a roaring success and the orchestra was given an enthusiastic reception wherever they went. Charles Groves took the orchestra back to Germany and Switzerland two years later. There were more tours to come and, in 1973, the orchestra appeared in Paris for the first time, along with the recently knighted Sir Charles. The French critics, such as Marc Pincherle in *Les Nouvelles Littéraires*, were full of praise:

> One of the best English orchestras, the Royal Liverpool Philharmonic, has just paid its first visit to Paris. It consists of almost a hundred musicians of high technical standard and remarkable cohesion. As is often the case in Great Britain the feminine element is widely represented, not only among the strings (the first cello is a woman) but among the woodwind, (two out of three oboes, three out of four flutes) and it also includes a woman percussionist. The brass are magnificent, notably the first trumpet. Their Conductor, Sir Charles Groves, genial and unassuming, reminiscent of Monteux, seems to have over his performers an authority based on complete confidence. He conducts austerely, efficiently, without the slightest attempt to curry favour with the public.

The RLPO continued to perform around Britain as well. Such was the popularity of the orchestra that the *Newcastle Sunday Sun* reported on 5th October 1969 that:

> Hundreds of ticketless fans stormed the City Hall last night in an effort to see their Merseyside favourites – the Liverpool Philharmonic Orchestra. Mr Michael Emmerson, director of the Newcastle Festival, said that they turned up hoping to buy tickets for the concert, which featured Beethoven's work … 'Newcastle has never before known such enthusiasm for a concert like this', said Mr. Emmerson.

To try to cope with the demand, the Festival's organisers scheduled an extra performance by the Phil and Sir Charles the following morning.

— en souvenir du magnifique concert du 12 mars 1968, où
fut donnée "Turangalîla-Symphonie" à Liverpool,
par Charles Groves (avec Yvonne Loriod & Jeanne Loriod
en soliste) & le Royal Liverpool Philharmonic Orchestra —
avec toute ma joie & ma reconnaissance !

Olivier Messiaen

Liverpool - 12 mars 1968 -

En souvenir très ému et reconnaissant
de ce beau concert Mozart-Messiaen !
Avec un énorme BRAVO pour
ce chef merveilleux de poésie,
de chaleur, de musique:
Charles GROVES!
et pour l'extraordinaire acoustique !

Avec toute ma grande
reconnaissance & mon admiration
Yvonne Loriod

Charles Groves

Jeanne Loriod

glad to have played
here again.

Segovia
1963

To Philharmonic Society

As a remembrance of
my concert with this wonderful Orchestra
and with my best wishes

Victoria de los Angeles

April 15-1969.

Messiaen

In March 1968, Groves conducted the Phil in a performance of Messiaen's *Turangalîla Symphony*, in the presence of the composer. Messiaen's wife performed on stage during the concert, which was broadcast live on the BBC Third Programme. The critics were, once again, full of praise for the performance.

Ronald Crichton wrote in the *Financial Times*:

> It was a resounding performance in every sense – seldom has one heard climaxes so full of warm and vibrant sound, approaching the level of tolerance but without harshness or coarseness, as those that crowned scherzo and finale. No less lovely in this admirable hall were the blissfully soupy sounds of the slow section …

Gerald Larner for *The Guardian* said:

> … the orchestral playing was magnificent, with an exciting virtuoso security …

And William Mann told readers of *The Times*:

> The whole performance … represented another triumph of grand enterprise by this orchestra which always plays with exemplary brio and musicality whenever I visit Liverpool to hear it …

Schoolboy Conductor

While Charles Groves was wowing the national critics, a 15-year-old Liverpool schoolboy was garnering plenty of local press coverage of his own. The teenager asked a local charity if he could put on a musical evening to raise funds for them. They were rather shocked five weeks later when he told them that he had drummed up a 70-piece orchestra from scratch. The name of this local lad might be familiar: Simon Rattle. At the time a pupil at Liverpool College, Sefton Park, he was a timpanist in the National Youth Orchestra and the Merseyside Youth Orchestra. He told the *Liverpool Echo*:

> I would like to make a career in music as a conductor and this is going to be a wonderful opportunity for me to conduct a symphony orchestra of such talents. They don't seem to mind my age.

The Merseyside Youth Orchestra performing in Lausanne in 1972.

Simon Rattle playing for the Merseyside Youth Orchestra in 1972.

A 15-year-old Simon Rattle rehearses his orchestra for a charity fundraiser.

April 27, 1970

Justin feels like a chat . . .

Everything stops for the leader of the band

FOUR - YEAR - OLD Justin Busbridge decided he wasn't playing second fiddle to one of Britain's youngest conductors, even if his mother was.

So he went to have a word with her. And that brought a momentary note of discord to the proceedings.

But conductor Simon Rattle, 15, had no intention of waving the big stick. He decided a diplomatic approach befitting his position was called for.

In true Sir Thomas Beecham style, he peered down from his podium and said: 'I see our leader has arrived.'

Justin was forgiven. He had helped break the ice for Simon and the 74-strong orchestra.

Simon, a sixth former at Liver-pool College, rounded up the musicians to play for the city's Spastic Fellowship and after five-and-a-half hours rehearsing they were full of praise for the young conductor.

The happy band included five players from the Royal Liverpool Philharmonic Orchestra, two Merseyside conductors and two of Simon's teachers.

. . . so he wanders over to the rostrum . . .

. . . where he gets a look of disapproval from conductor Simon Rattle.

Liverpool Philharmonic Youth Orchestra

The Liverpool Philharmonic Youth Orchestra began its life as the Merseyside Youth Orchestra in 1951, as part of the Festival of Britain. The driving force behind the orchestra for its first twenty-two years was its conductor, William Jenkins, who was also Music Adviser to the Liverpool Education Committee. The orchestra's first performance was the Overture to Mozart's opera *The Magic Flute.* Since 1972, the Royal Liverpool Philharmonic Society has administered the orchestra and, in 2006, during its 55th anniversary year, its name was changed to the Liverpool Philharmonic Youth Orchestra, re-emphasising the close links and prestige association of its young musicians with the RLPO and Philharmonic Hall.

The orchestra's most famous alumnus is that Liverpool College old boy, Sir Simon Rattle, who was a percussionist in the MYO from 1965 to 1972. Now the orchestra's Patron, he is convinced that being a part of the orchestra helped him on the road to international success:

> The Orchestra has an unequalled record in producing professional musicians; there are members in almost all of the British Orchestras and many abroad – indeed some orchestras are almost saturated with Scousers! For all of us, it was a musical lifeline, and enabled us to play to a high standard very early – still rare in England. If the Arts are to survive in Great Britain, they must be nurtured from the roots up – and this orchestra has proved to be one of the most fertile seeds in English music.

The Liverpool Philharmonic Youth Orchestra performs four concerts each season at Philharmonic Hall. It is also invited to give concerts in community settings, as well as providing small ensembles for functions and events. The orchestra is committed to international touring and has performed in many countries worldwide, including Poland, Spain, Germany, Hungary and the Czech Republic. Its Principal Conductor is Matthew Wood.

All Change at the Phil

Today's Liverpool Philharmonic
Youth Orchestra in rehearsal.

When Sir Charles Groves decided to lay down his baton, it marked the end of a remarkably successful period for the orchestra. His fourteen years in charge had seen the orchestra's profile rise in both the national and international classical music arenas. Both Sir John Pritchard and Sir Charles Groves had performed an impressive number of UK and world premieres during their tenures. Among Pritchard's seventeen first performances were works by Walton, Arnold, Henze, Maxwell Davies and Goehr. Groves's debuts included works by Walton, Mathias, Lutoslawski, McCabe, Rubbra, Berio and even Shostakovich. Overseas tours and a strong catalogue of recordings had helped to spread the reputation of the orchestra far and wide. It was always going to be hard to replace a man who had enjoyed so much success over a fourteen-year term. Now, the Phil was to enter a period where it was to have three Principal Conductors in quick succession, with none sticking around in the top job for more than three years.

Walter Weller

Born: Vienna, 1939
Principal Conductor: 1977–1980

A violin prodigy, Walter Weller followed his father into the Vienna Philharmonic Orchestra. By the time he was just twenty-one years old, he was appointed joint concert master with Willi Boskovsky. Shortly afterwards he established a string quartet, which received international acclaim. From 1969 onwards, he conducted regularly at the Vienna Volksoper and the Vienna State Opera. After his three years as Principal Conductor of the RLPO from 1977 to 1980, he spent six years with the Royal Philharmonic Orchestra. He was Principal Conductor of the Royal Scottish National Orchestra between 1991 and 1996 and is currently Music Director of the National Orchestra of Belgium. He is an accomplished amateur magician and a model railway enthusiast.

Walter Weller conducted his first dates with the Royal Liverpool Philharmonic in 1975 and returned two years later as Principal Conductor. By the 1970s, modern symphony orchestras spent far less time with their main conductors than they did in the days of Sargent. In his first season, Weller conducted the orchestra fourteen times and in his second and third seasons, he was contracted for thirty concerts each year.

At the beginning of his tenure in 1977, he gave an interview to the indomitable Joe Riley, then the Arts Correspondent – and now the retired Arts Editor – of the *Liverpool Echo*. It seemed clear that Weller was only planning to stay with the Phil for the duration of his three year contract. He said:

> I like the people and the place. The orchestra has a good tone. I'm sure that I shall enjoy the next three years very much. Ever since I first conducted here, two years ago, my engagements with the orchestra have been most memorable.

In July and August of 1979, Weller led the RLPO and the RLPC on a tour of Yugoslavia and Austria. The orchestra was a big hit, gaining rave reviews and being compared very favourably to the leading European orchestras of the time. The critic from *Kleine Zeitung* wrote:

> At last a top flight orchestra has appeared again at the Carinthian Summer Festival. Liverpool, the musical birthplace of The Beatles, has with its Royal Liverpool Philharmonic Orchestra splendid things to offer the realm of classical music. In Tchaikovsky's musical reworking of the tragic love story of *Romeo and Juliet* the English players brought out to the full the illuminating power of this brilliant fantasy overture. All the instrumental groups of this huge orchestra played outstandingly well. First class string players provided the intensive shaping of the dramatic action. Secure woodwind and radiant brass produced tremendous climaxes within the work.

Weller was a far from radical Principal Conductor. During his time with the Phil, he opted instead to develop the standard of the orchestra's playing of the more traditional end of the repertoire. There were far fewer contemporary music surprises than there had been in the days of Pritchard and Groves. Instead, his concerts tended to follow the more conservative format of an overture, followed by a concerto, with a symphony to finish. However, during this period, the still young Simon Rattle returned to his home city to conduct the orchestra, bringing with him a more contemporary outlook to his programming choices.

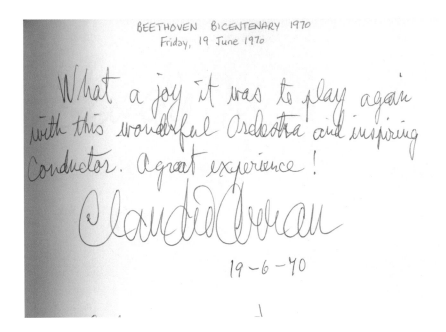

BEETHOVEN BICENTENARY 1970
Friday, 19 June 1970

What a joy it was to play again with this wonderful Orchestra and inspiring Conductor. A great experience!

Claudio Arrau

19-6-70

WEEK-END SERIES
Saturday, 4 May, 1974

C'était une soirée Très spéciale! Avec mes meilleurs sentiments!

Martha Argerich

74

yes indeed!

Charles Dutoit

4 May 74

Above. Autograph of Claudio Arrau, the distinguished Chilean pianist.

Above right. Another great pianist, Martha Argerich, signs the Phil's autograph book, alongside her then husband, conductor Charles Dutoit.

Right. Programme of a recital in 1980 by Phil regular Yehudi Menuhin.

Below. Autograph of great Russian violinist David Oistrakh.

Royal Liverpool Philharmonic Society

R**L**PS

Recital

Yehudi Menuhin
Louis Kentner

15 May 1980 at 7.30

WEEK-END SERIES
Sunday, 3 December, 1972

Сердечно приветствую и благодарю!
Ваш Очень
/David Oistrakh/

David Atherton

Born: Blackpool, 1944
Principal Conductor: 1980–1983

David Atherton was the closest thing to home–grown talent among the Liverpool Phil's Principal Conductors since the Society's foundation back in 1840. Although, he was not born on Merseyside, Blackpool is certainly in the geographical catchment area that The Royal Liverpool Philharmonic considers its own. The RLPO was the first orchestra he heard live, when he was taken to one of the Phil's regular concerts in Preston. After studying music at Cambridge University, Atherton was the youngest ever conductor to appear at the Royal Opera House, where he was resident for twelve years. The co–founder of the London Sinfonietta, he was also, at the time, the youngest conductor to appear at the BBC Proms Concerts. He combined his role at Liverpool with the Music Directorship of the San Diego Symphony Orchestra, where he stayed until 1987. He was Music Director of the Hong Kong Philharmonic from 1989 to 2000.

During David Atherton's three year stint as Principal Conductor, the orchestra powered ahead. There were successful tours of Germany in 1980 and 1981. When the Phil played in Berlin, the newspaper *Der Tages Spiegel* reported:

> Liverpool, the home of the Beatles, is also the home of an orchestra that, as its Gala performance in the Philharmonie confirmed, deserves to be ranked as one of the leading international orchestras … Wild applause and shouts of bravo expressed the audience's gratitude for this interpretation, one which was again a reminder that perfection and feeling can go hand in hand.

And the critic from the *Berliner Morgenpost* was even more impressed:

> The Royal Liverpool Philharmonic gave us a tremendous surprise. It taught us that, even outside London, English musical life has made astounding progress. England in the last decades has really become a wonderland of continuous surprises in the world of music.
>
> The Liverpool Orchestra is not a new foundation. It is, in fact, much older than our own Philharmonic. It was as early as 1840 that the Liverpool Philharmonic Society was founded and the Orchestra bears the same name. So it is one of the oldest orchestras in the world.
>
> But on the platform it impresses one as being delightfully young. It plays with verve, with power and with confidence. It has very pronounced artistic élan, which conveys its spontaneity to the audience. One does not want to say that it was just highly polished orchestral playing. All sections of the orchestra have far more than mere individual skills. They all play their own brilliant part in the context of the complete orchestra.

Also in 1981, for the only time in its history, the RLPO spent a month in London, performing at the Royal Opera House, Covent Garden, as the resident orchestra for the Royal Ballet's 50th anniversary celebrations.

1981 was a difficult year for Liverpool as a City, with violent riots breaking out over a nine day period in the Toxteth area. The Philharmonic Hall, in Hope Street, is on the very edge of Toxteth. To reassure concertgoers during this period, the Society launched the 'Philharmonic Shuttle' – a bus which took people from city centre car parks to the door of the Philharmonic Hall. Equally important in encouraging concert-goers back into the Hall in daylight hours was a series of lunchtime concerts, for which the players received no money at first.

Composer in Residence

In 1983, Edward Cowie was given the role as 'Composer in Residence' to the Royal Liverpool Philharmonic. It was the first time that a composer had been embedded in the life of a major British orchestra. As part of the three-year project, much of his work centred around taking classical music into the community, but he also wrote a symphony for the RLPO and a new work for the Merseyside Youth Orchestra. He told Joe Riley in the *Liverpool Echo* that his appointment would be 'like going back to the 19th century Viennese composers, who had a remarkably close relationship with their patrons, and produced music dove-tailed to their needs.' Other composers have followed Cowie in enjoying close – and artistically fruitful – relationships with the Phil, including Graham Fitkin, Django Bates, David Horne and Kenneth Hesketh.

Marek Janowski

Born: Warsaw, 1939
Artistic Advisor /
Principal Conductor: 1983-1987

Although Polish by birth, Marek Janowski grew up in Germany. His main roles have included Music Director of the Orchestre Philharmonique de Radio France from 1984 to 2000; Kapellmeister of the Gürzenich Orchestra, Cologne between 1986 and 1990; Principal Conductor of the Monte Carlo Philharmonic from 2000 to 2005 and Principal Conductor of the Dresden Philharmonic from 2001 to 2004. Since 2002, he has been Principal Conductor of the Berlin Radio Symphony Orchestra, as well as being Director of the Orchestre de la Suisse Romande from 2005 onwards.

At the beginning of the 1983 season, David Atherton and Marek Janowski effectively swapped jobs. Janowski had been the Phil's Principal Guest Conductor since 1980. Atherton moved to this new role and Janowski took the more senior position. Interestingly though, he was not officially given the title of Principal Conductor, instead being referred to merely as 'Artistic Advisor'. It was agreed that with Janowski only being in Liverpool for twenty concerts per year, his time commitment was not great enough for him to be given the usual title. To make up the shortfall, Walter Weller retained his links with the orchestra, under the title Guest Conductor Laureate, as he had done through Atherton's time in charge.

Janowski was presented to the Liverpool public as a Wagner expert with a love of Messiaen – on paper the perfect balance between Weller, who was more conservative in his programming, and Atherton, the more adventurous.

Under Threat

Janowski's three years at the orchestra's helm were somewhat overshadowed by financial uncertainty. In 1986, the abolition of Merseyside County Council led to the very real threat that the Royal Liverpool Philharmonic was just weeks away from closing altogether. The Council owned and funded the Philharmonic Hall, but only days before it was to be abolished, there was still no clear commitment to the orchestra's future. A major campaign was launched to save the orchestra, led by the players. Principal Horn, Jim Dowling, and Timpanist, Ian Wright, delivered a petition containing 106,200 signatures to Liverpool City Council. It was part of a sustained campaign by the players that even involved performing on the streets of Liverpool in full evening dress. The protests gained national media attention and undoubtedly helped to move the plight of the Liverpool Phil up the agenda of music and arts lovers outside of the City itself.

Under the local government changes, the City Council, which at the time was dominated by Labour's Militant wing, needed to stump up the largest part of the funding, although all of the districts in the area which was formerly controlled by Merseyside County Council, also needed to pledge funding to the orchestra to keep

The RLPO campaigning to save the
Phil in 1986.

The RLPO's brass section playing
their part in the campaign.

Principal Horn Jim Dowling and
Timpanist Ian Wright presenting
the petition of 106,200 signatures
to save the Phil.

it going. It was a far cry from the days of the old Liverpool City Council in the post-war years, which saw the orchestra as a source of municipal pride.

Eventually, after much wrangling, closure was prevented. The ownership of the Hall was transferred to the Merseyside Residuary Body. In a written reply in the House of Commons to a question tabled by Ken Hind, the Conservative MP for Lancashire West, the Arts Minister Richard Luce said:

> The Royal Liverpool Philharmonic Society is currently establishing a charitable trust which could subsequently be responsible for the hall. I am sure the Residuary Body will wish to consult the trust and other interested parties before deciding on final arrangements for the ownership and management of the hall.

He added that he hoped the longer-term future of the Hall would be secured with continuing assistance from the Arts Council, the five district councils and, wherever possible, the private sector.

The charitable trust did indeed come into being and a lease was signed for the Hall in March 1988. The Royal Liverpool Philharmonic was back in control of its own destiny.

Stephen Gray OBE served as General Manager of the Phil from 1964 to 1987. On 29th August 1987, a unique gala concert was given to mark his retirement. The five Principal Conductors Stephen worked with during twenty-three years all took part, as did Simon Rattle, whose talent he had encouraged.

Back row: (left to right) Simon Rattle, Walter Weller, Brian Pidgeon (general manager), Marek Janowski, David Atherton. Front row: Sir Charles Groves, Stephen Gray, Libor Pešek.

Chapter Seven

The Best Czech Orchestra This Side of Prague

Genna Spinks. Double Bass, Royal Liverpool
Philharmonic Orchestra. Photographed at St. George's
Hall, Liverpool.

By arrangement with Harold Shaw and in association with IMG Artists (Europe)

Royal Liverpool Philharmonic Orchestra

Libor Pešek *Music Director*

A New Hero

The appointment of Libor Pešek as the RLPO's new Principal Conductor in 1987 was inspired. Although he had only conducted the orchestra twice before the appointment was made, he immediately struck up a strong rapport with the players and was quickly taken to the hearts of the Phil's faithful audience. His charm was apparent from the start, as reported by the *Liverpool Daily Post*'s long-serving Arts Editor, Philip Key, in July 1986, when Pešek was introduced to the press for the first time:

> With his film star looks, easy manner and relaxed attitude to life, Libor Pešek is the sort of chap to make birds fall out of trees … Surprisingly he began by announcing that when offered the job 'my first reaction was negative'. It seems he did not feel like taking on the responsibility and wanted 'just to be myself'. But then he recalled the orchestra's positive attitude to a work new to them (and, incidentally, Pešek himself). It was a difficult piece, he said, but they worked hard together and showed a professionalism 'in the best sense of the word'. Above all, they showed they still have a love of playing music, something not always apparent with other orchestras. 'So I thought how good it would be to once more make a communion with them.' He accepted the job.

Libor Pešek KBE

Born: Prague, 1933
Principal Conductor: 1987-1997

Libor Pešek studied conducting, piano, cello and trombone at Prague's Academy of Music and Arts. From 1958 to 1964, he was the founding director of the Prague Chamber Harmony. For a year from 1981, he was Chief Conductor of the Slovak Philharmonic before spending nine years as the Conductor-in-Residence of the Czech Philharmonic Orchestra between 1982 and 1991. He became Music Director of the Royal Liverpool Philharmonic Orchestra in 1987. After ten years with the orchestra, he gave up the principal conducting role, but remains the Orchestra's Conductor Laureate. Pešek has helped to make Czech music famous the world over, particularly through his recordings with the Czech Philharmonic and with the RLPO. He is a major supporter of the music of his fellow countrymen: Suk, Dvořák, Novák and Janáček. He was awarded the KBE in 1996.

During the decade that Libor Pešek spent as the Liverpool Phil's Music Director, he helped to build up the orchestra's reputation, not least in Europe, where he conducted it on a series of tours. He relished taking the Liverpool players to his home city of Prague and showing off their skill as interpreters of the music of his homeland. Indeed, the RLPO earned the sobriquet, 'The best Czech orchestra this side of Prague'. The orchestra honed these skills back home and the ears of Liverpool's concert-going public were opened up to new repertoire from Central Europe during Pešek's period in charge. However, he was not exclusively a Czech conductor and his concerts also included English composers, such as Elgar, Vaughan Williams and Britten, alongside more familiar German Romantic works.

Pešek threw himself into Liverpool life, basing himself in Liverpool for long periods and appearing with the orchestra not just at the Philharmonic Hall, but also on 'out of town' concerts in regular venues such as Preston and Blackburn.

Just three years into his tenure, Pešek had proven to be an enormous hit and had developed a devoted fan-club on Merseyside. When the Royal Liverpool Philharmonic Society celebrated its 150th anniversary, the *Liverpool Echo* praised its Music Director for giving the Phil 'new strengths':

> He has the rugged good looks of a film star, the charm of a gentleman, the life-loving qualities of a bon viveur and the good humour of a practised conversationalist. But beneath the obvious qualities of the Phil's Music Director, Libor Pešek, is a gritty determination which has raised his orchestra to new strengths and a glittery future.

Pešek helped to secure a series of recording deals for the Phil, with eleven albums being recorded for the EMI and Virgin labels in one year alone – far greater than the orchestra's output in the years leading up to Pešek's arrival.

Later in the year, the *Liverpool Echo* trumpeted the line-up for the Phil's 1990-1991 season with the words:

> The Royal Liverpool Philharmonic Orchestra is enjoying something of a Golden Era. It just so happens that its 150th birthday, this year, has

180

181

Happy Birthday Phil !

1990·91 Season at the Philharmonic Hall

ROYAL LIVERPOOL PHILHARMONIC
1840 1990

Celebrating 150 years of Music on Merseyside

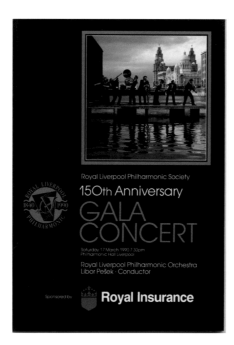

Royal Liverpool Philharmonic Society
150th Anniversary GALA CONCERT

Saturday 17 March 1990 7.30pm
Philharmonic Hall Liverpool

Royal Liverpool Philharmonic Orchestra
Libor Pešek · Conductor

Sponsored by
Royal Insurance

FESTIVAL DE LILLE 92

PAUL McCARTNEY'S LIVERPOOL ORATORIO

Paul McCartney's
LIVERPOOL ORATORIO
per Paul McCartney i Carl Davis.

Carl Davis director
Barbara Bonney soprano
David Rendall tenor
Sally Burgess contralt
Jonathan Summers baix
Jeremy Budd noi solista

Royal Liverpool Philharmonic Orchestra & Choir
Choristers of Liverpool Cathedral

Dia 22 de maig de 1992 a les 22'00
Palau Sant Jordi de Barcelona

Harrison/Parrot Ltd. London
coordinadors del concert

FUNDACIÓ CATALANA SÍNDROME DE DOWN

Wednesday Series
31 January 1990

Thank you again —
the orchestra sound
fabulous !

Stephen Hays

Valery Gergiev
(with love!)

Wednesday Series
11 December 1991

Chaxian
Vengerov.

Paul McCartney's
Liverpool Oratorio
Première at Liverpool Cathedral 28/29 June 1991

coincided with some of the orchestra's best playing in its history. Critics have sat up and taken notice and the orchestra's reputation across Europe and the world is at an all-time high. Recording activities have increased, along with concert audiences, and there is a fresh, eager spirit within the ranks. Much of this is thanks to its Czech-born music director Libor Pešek whose own reputation has risen with that of the orchestra.

Pešek joined with Jean Boht (Ma Boswell from the TV series *Bread* – and, incidentally, the wife of the long-time Phil favourite, Carl Davis) at Lime Street Station for the unveiling of a locomotive to be named 'The Liverpool Phil' in honour of the Society's 150th anniversary. The Orchestra and Choir then travelled down to London for a 150th Anniversary Gala Concert at The Barbican Centre. There was an anxious moment or two when the train was delayed for seventy-five minutes because of a signal problem, but the concert passed off without a hitch.

The eminent music critic Michael Kennedy, writing in the *Daily Telegraph*, praised the output of the orchestra in its anniversary year:

> In Liverpool, the RLPO celebrates its 150th season with a characteristically wide-ranging series, including the first performance next January of Robert Simpson's 10th Symphony and such enticing occasions as Maxwell Davies conducting two of his own works; Libor Pešek conducting Elgar's 2nd Symphony; Sir Charles Groves conducting Birtwistle's *The Triumph of Time* and Tippett's *Triple Concerto*, Schnittke's *Piano Concerto* played by Peter Frankl with Paul Daniel conducting, Mahler's 2nd, 4th and 7th Symphonies and *Das Lied von der Erde*, and such English classics as Howells' *Hymnus Paradisi* and Vaughan Williams' *Pastoral* and 4th Symphonies.

Another major event that year was the première of *Paul McCartney's Liverpool Oratorio* in Liverpool Cathedral. The orchestra's performance, which gained worldwide media attention, was conducted by Carl Davis, who worked on the orchestration with McCartney.

The subscription brochure for the Phil's 150th anniversary season.

A Gala Concert celebrating 150 years of the Liverpool Philharmonic.

The RLPO performed the *Liverpool Oratorio* successfully around the world, including these performances in Lille and Barcelona.

Autograph of Valery Gergiev, on the famous Russian conductor's only visit to Liverpool to date.

Autograph of the great Russian violinist Maxim Vengerov on his Liverpool debut, aged 17.

Autograph of Paul McCartney on the première of his *Liverpool Oratorio*.

Royal Choir

As part of the Society's 150th birthday celebrations, the Queen conferred patronage on the Liverpool Philharmonic Choir, which then became known as the Royal Liverpool Philharmonic Choir. The Society and the Orchestra had enjoyed Royal patronage since 1957. Ian Tracey took over as the Choir's Chorus Master in 1985, a role that he retains today. He is credited with raising standards in the choir and dramatically increasing the number of concerts and recordings that it makes.

The RLPC's history dates back to the very beginnings of the Royal Liverpool Philharmonic Society. Dr J.E. Wallace was its longest-serving Chorus Master, staying in the role from 1929 to 1970, apart from a brief wartime interlude. The choir had a fractious relationship with one or two of the Society's earliest Principal Conductors and in 1923, Sir Henry Wood decided that despite two years of solid rehearsals, the choir was unable to sing Bach's *B minor Mass* well enough for it to be performed in public. The exasperated conductor forced them to go away to practise for another six months. However, under the tutelage of Sir Malcolm Sargent during the Second World War, the choir flourished. Today, the Royal Liverpool Philharmonic Choir is in great demand.

The Phil offers other inspiring opportunities to take part in singing. Liverpool Philharmonic Youth Choir, directed by Simon Emery, is one of the North West's finest youth choirs offering young singers exceptional training and performance experience including performing and recording with the RLPO. Younger singers in Liverpool Philharmonic Training Choir and Melody Makers can progress to the Youth Choir.

Liverpool Philharmonic Gospel Choir has gained a reputation for exciting and inspirational performances under the direction of renowned Gospel musician, Tyndale Thomas.

Liverpool Philharmonic Community Choir is a non-auditioning choir suitable for anyone with a love of singing. Led by Gareth Owen, its repertoire covers pop to rock, folk to classical, world music to jazz.

Liverpool Philharmonic
Youth Choir.

Royal Liverpool Philharmonic
Choir today, with Vasily
Petrenko and Chorus Master
Ian Tracey.

Liverpool Philharmonic
Gospel Choir.

Liverpool Philharmonic
Community Choir.

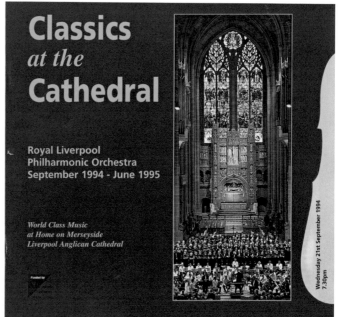

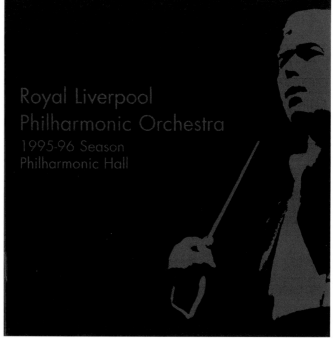

The first concert in the refurbished
Philharmonic Hall.

Concert programme for one of the
concerts held at Liverpool Cathedral.

The syllabus for the first season at the
refurbished Hall.

A New Look for the Hall

The art deco splendour of Philharmonic Hall was restored in 1995, following a £10.3 million refurbishment. The orchestra transferred to Liverpool's Anglican Cathedral for a year, while the work was done. This offered the opportunity to present a season of concerts specifically chosen to fill this huge enclosed space.

Handing Over the Baton

In 1997, Libor Pešek decided to relinquish his Music Directorship of the Liverpool Phil, although he continues his love affair with the City to the present day in his role as Conductor Laureate. In an interview with the *Daily Telegraph* in May 1997, he was in reflective mood about his time with the orchestra:

> When I first saw Liverpool it was a disrupted city. It reflected my soul. The City was in shambles, my soul was in a shambles. We have much in common. Liverpudlians are emotional people and a loyal public. They helped us survive … After two concerts the orchestra proposed to me. I was 53 on the brink of old age. Funnily enough I was; and this orchestra has made me young again.

Petr Altrichter

Born: Frenštát pod Radhoštěm
Czech Republic, 1951
Principal Conductor: 1997–2001

Petr Altrichter studied the French horn and conducting at the Ostrava Music Conservatoire. He also studied at the Janáček Academy of Music and Performing Arts. He was first Principal Guest Conductor and, from 1990 to 1992, Principal Conductor of the Prague Symphony Orchestra. From 1993 to 2004, he was Music Director of the Südwestdeutsche Philharmonie. Since 2002, he has been the Principal Conductor of the Brno Philharmonic Orchestra.

Libor Pešek's reign as Music Director ended with a Gala Concert. Pešek had introduced a number of unknown Czech artists to Liverpool during his ten years with the orchestra. None had galvanized the players quite so much as the conductor Petr Altrichter. When it came to choosing a replacement for Pešek, Altrichter received the unanimous backing of the orchestra.

Although unknown in this country and without the big record deal that it was customary for Principal Conductors to have at the time, he looked set to be the man to continue the work that Pešek had begun.

Altrichter began his first season in September 1997 with Haydn's *Creation* and ended it with Janáček's *Glagolitic Mass*. One of the season's highlights was the 'Out of the Shadows' Festival, directed by Kathryn Stott and featuring the music of the neglected female composers Fanny Mendelssohn and Clara Schumann. The RLPO returned to the Royal Albert Hall for the BBC Proms and a performance of the Poulenc *Organ Concerto*, with Ian Tracey as the soloist. Deborah Warner directed a semi-staged performance of Honegger's *Joan of Arc*. The Summer Pops season at the King's Dock was the most successful to date, with 35,000 people attending thirteen concerts conducted by Carl Davis.

Money worries have never been too far away in the Phil's history. The organisation had suffered the consequences of the decline in the Liverpool economy through the 1970s and 1980s and the recession in the early 1990s, as well as the abolition of the Metropolitan County Council in 1986. Insolvency was at times a very real risk, but in 1999, the Royal Liverpool Philharmonic made a successful application to Arts Council England's Stabilisation Scheme. As had happened in the past, there was a strange contradiction of continuing financial worries behind the scenes in stark contrast to the vibrant artistic programme on the platform.

In July, 2000, Arts Council England ratified the Stabilisation Unit's initial decision to award the Royal Liverpool Philharmonic £5.4 million, with the possibility of a further award once the Society had moved along the pathway towards standing on its own two feet in economic terms.

As a result of the stabilisation funding, the entire organisation behind the scenes at the Liverpool Phil was overhauled under the newly appointed Chief Executive, Michael Elliott. With a background in publicly funded arts management, he turned out to be the perfect man for the delicate job of allowing the orchestra to develop artistically, while at the same making sure the business part of the organisation delivered the financial numbers necessary to continue operating.

RLPO Live

Although many people in the classical music world will tell you that the London Symphony Orchestra was the first British orchestra to own and run its own record label, the honour actually fell to the Royal Liverpool Philharmonic. RLPO Live was born in 1998 at the initiative of the musicians of the orchestra, in response to the decline in core classical orchestral CD sales from the major record companies. Using technical expertise from within the orchestra, and with the support of the Musicians' Union, a new company was formed in which all performers, including the conductor and soloist, were equal shareholders. The principle was based on recording live concerts and selling them, initially to a local market, but ultimately to wider audiences.

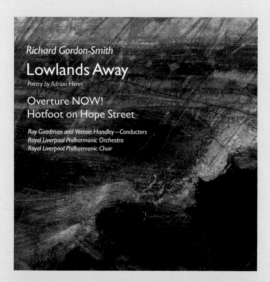

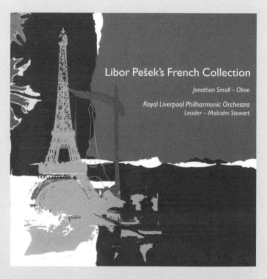

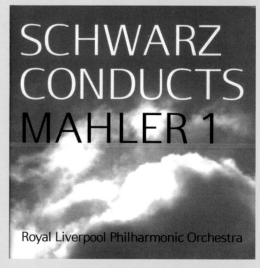

Ensemble 10/10

Ensemble 10/10 is another example of a great idea that was born from within the orchestra itself. Described by *The Times* as 'The Royal Liverpool Philharmonic's avant-garde flying squad', this contemporary music ensemble was founded in 1997 by cellist Hilary Browning and clarinettist Nicholas Cox. Since its launch, the group has flourished and has given dozens of world première performances. Working under its conductor Clark Rundell, Ensemble 10/10's recent commissions have included works from composers such as Graham Fitkin, Steve Martland, Ian Gardiner, James Wishart, Michael Torke, Stephen Pratt, Ian Stephens and Kenneth Hesketh. Many of the performances take place in the excellent acoustic of The Cornerstone, Hope at Everton — part of Liverpool Hope University, which is now a significant educational partner with the Royal Liverpool Philharmonic.

In the 2007/08 season, Ensemble 10/10 celebrated their 10th anniversary by commissioning ten, ten-minute works, which were performed in a special birthday concert in November 2007, following individual performances of each work during the anniversary season.

There followed a period of rapid and – at times painful – change as the organisation sought to balance the books. A series of strong chairmen in the shape of Peter Toyne, Roger Lewis and Lorraine Rogers spent the next few years working with Elliott to negotiate with funders to ensure the future of the orchestra.

Petr Altrichter was proving to be a great success with the baton and his three year contract was quickly extended to 2001. Gerard Schwarz was one of a number of guest conductors; his two-week period of concerts in the 1998-1999 season brought with them a sense of innovation. As well as producing superb concerts, communicating well to both the audience and the orchestra, he brought many new ideas from his own orchestra in Seattle. He was quickly marked out as a man to be invited back.

One particular star on the platform in the 1999-2000 season was 12-year-old Marie-Elisabeth Lott, who caused such a storm with Paganini's *Violin Concerto No. 1* that the interval had to be extended to allow the audience to get autographs.

The 2000-2001 season was the last for Petr Altrichter. Given Liverpool's links to the USA over the years, it seems remarkable that the orchestra had not looked across the pond for a Principal Conductor before 2001.

On the platform, the first season under Gerard Schwarz (2001-2002) started with a real sense of buzz following an extraordinarily successful performance of Mahler's *Symphony No. 2*, which was broadcast on BBC Radio 3. It was a particularly difficult occasion for the Phil's new Music Director – not only was he conducting his new orchestra for the first time, but the concert came barely thirty hours after the terrorist attacks on the World Trade Centre in Schwarz's home city of New York.

Schwarz's first season culminated in a formidable performance at the BBC Proms and the whole organisation felt as though it was on a roll. Liverpool City Council recognised the value that the orchestra brought to the City by deciding to award an 800% increase in its annual grant to the Society. The combination of the successful Arts Council Stabilisation programme and the major increase in City Council support changed the fortunes of the Liverpool Phil beyond recognition.

Gerard Schwarz

Born: Weehawken, New Jersey, 1947
Music Director: 2001-2006

Gerard Schwarz was born in New Jersey to Austrian parents. After graduating from the Juilliard School, he began his professional music career as a trumpeter, rising to become Principal of the New York Philharmonic Orchestra. He began conducting in 1966 and was Music Director of the Los Angeles Chamber Orchestra from 1978 to 1986. He led New York's Mostly Mozart Festival as Music Director from 1982 to 2001 and became Music Director of the Seattle Symphony Orchestra in 1985 – a post he continues to hold today, as well as being Music Advisor and Principal Conductor of the Eastern Music Festival. He has recorded extensively with a number of orchestras around the world and produced a critically acclaimed series of Mahler symphonies with the RLPO.

Classic FM

To coincide with the arrival of the new Music Director, the Royal Liverpool
Philharmonic entered into a ground-breaking partnership with the UK's leading
classical music station, Classic FM. Originally established for three years, the
partnership has been extend to 2012 and continues to raise the profile of the
orchestra in Liverpool, regionally and throughout the UK.

The original partnership was born out of a shared desire to build new audiences for
classical music. In a unique piece of market research, commissioned by the Royal
Liverpool Philharmonic in 2005, and the biggest survey of its kind undertaken by a
UK orchestra, the partnership was identified as a major factor in encouraging people
to try live classical music. 88% of those questioned had heard a Liverpool Phil feature
on Classic FM and 23% had booked tickets for concerts as a result.

The Classic FM Series of concerts at the Philharmonic Hall features popular and
accessible music from the repertoire, while the orchestra's recordings regularly
feature on the Classic FM playlist. At the beginning of 2008, the station
announced that it would broadcast 25 exclusively recorded concert performances
by the Liverpool Phil.

Backing the Bid

On 4th June 2003, the Government announced that Liverpool would be the European Capital of Culture in 2008. The same evening, the Royal Liverpool Philharmonic Orchestra and Choir celebrated this achievement with the performance of a fanfare composed during that day by Ian Stephens. The campaign to persuade the selection committee that Liverpool should win the battle to be Capital of Culture had been fierce. Walking around the City in the weeks leading up to the decision, there could be no doubt that there was an overwhelmingly strong sense of desire from the people of Liverpool that their city should be chosen.

Celebrating the announcement of Liverpool as European Capital of Culture with cultural partners are Liverpool MP Louise Ellman, the Lord Mayor, Cllr Ron Gould, Liverpool City Council Chief Executive and Leader, Sir David Henshaw and Cllr Mike Storey, and Sir Bob Scott.

Learning & Engagement

The Royal Liverpool Philharmonic has been working with schools and the community through its orchestral programme since the 1940s, when Sir Malcolm Sargent first introduced a concert series for schools. Since then the programme has developed to offer a range of inspirational and exciting opportunities to enjoy and to take part in live music-making of the highest quality. These have been widely acclaimed locally, regionally and nationally.

The Learning team, which is led by Executive Director (Learning and Engagement) Peter Garden, works with other cultural partners, children's centres, schools, universities, local authorities and health and regeneration agencies to connect people and communities to the Royal Liverpool Philharmonic Orchestra, Philharmonic Hall and its wide-ranging music programme. Today, the programmes benefit more than 45,000 people in the North West region, including 22,000 young people each year.

The Phil has ambitious plans to expand its learning and engagement activities over the coming years. It aims to provide more opportunities to take part in music-making on a broad scale, while at the same time supporting the most talented young musicians in the region.

This transformation is already underway with the Phil playing a major role in the *Find Your Talent* programme, a national initiative to enable all young people under the age of nineteen to have access to the best cultural activities for five hours per week. In 2008, the Phil also successfully bid to win one of the three national pilots for the Department of Children, Schools and Families' *In Harmony* scheme. This project will deliver an intensive music programme to children in West Everton, one of the most deprived wards in England.

In Harmony, which is inspired by the hugely successful Venezuelan project 'El Sistema', will make music part of the children's everyday life.

The Phil's Family Concerts have developed a strong following and, in his *Daily Telegraph* column, Julian Lloyd Webber nominated them as No.1 in '21 reasons to be cheerful about classical music.'

A School Concert conducted by Louis Cohen in the 1940s.

A young Music for Life participant.

Young double bassists from the Phil's Music for Life project.

Music for Life

Launched in 2003, Music for Life is a visionary project helping to transform lives in the Kensington area of north Liverpool, one of the most deprived areas of the country. This award-winning programme, which sees the Phil resident in the area, involves children from five primary schools and their extended communities.

Music for Life contributes to the Kensington community on many different levels, including providing schools with instruments and adopted musicians and supporting a children's string orchestra and a community choir. The project has been described by Ofsted as 'exceptional' and named as a RENEW North West Exemplar Learning Programme in 2007 for its contribution to community regeneration.

Schools' Concerts

More than 17,500 school-age children and 2,300 teachers take part in the Phil's annual series of Schools' Concerts. These concerts are a fun and lively way to introduce children to live orchestral music, whilst providing teacher training and a comprehensive scheme of work to enhance the national curriculum. They have been part of the City's musical life for the past seven decades.

In October 2008, the Phil's Learning and Engagement programmes were showcased at a special reception at the House of Commons hosted by Jane Kennedy, MP for Liverpool Wavertree, and attended by the Secretary of State for Culture, Media and Sport, Andy Burnham, as well as more than one hundred MPs and Peers.

A schools' concert presented by Alasdair Malloy.

A musical encounter at the Phil.

Andy Burnham MP and Jane Kennedy MP with children from the Phil's Music for Life project.

Liverpool Philharmonic Hall

Today, Philharmonic Hall presents around 250 events each year, of which more than sixty are concerts by the Royal Liverpool Philharmonic Orchestra, selling approximately 250,000 tickets annually. The Hall is recognised as one of the UK's premier venues with an illustrious tradition of bringing the top names in rock, pop, jazz, roots, classical and contemporary music to Liverpool. Buddy Holly appeared there early on in his career. More recent appearances have included Blondie, Sigur Rós, Nitin Sawhney, Joan Baez, Willy Nelson, Tony Bennett, Morrissey, Van Morrison and Christy Moore.

The Hall also features comedy, with Jackie Mason, Dylan Moran, Jimmy Carr and Dara O'Briain having played there recently, while the annual marathon performances by Ken Dodd are a firm fixture in the Liverpool comedy diary. Films are shown on the Walturdaw cinema screen, accompanied by resident organist Dave Nicholas. After a significant investment in the Hall's sound system, the Liverpool Phil is now able to record and archive all of its concerts. The Hall's diverse programming was a central part of the 2008 European Capital of Culture celebrations and the team who manage the Hall, led by the Executive Director (Hall & Events) Simon Glinn, have also developed a string of creative partnerships with festivals, broadcasters and promoters. Innovative approaches to classical and non-classical programming include the presentation of acclaimed collaborations between the RLPO and international artists such as Amal Murkus, Marcel Khalife, Elvis Costello and Toumani Diabaté.

The Philharmonic Hall team is currently a significant partner in the programming, marketing and management of the spectacular St George's Hall Concert Room, and has responsibility for the operations management of the Phil's new rehearsal and recording venue at a former church in North Liverpool, now known as *Liverpool Phil at the Friary*.

Chapter Eight
The European Capital of Culture

Sally Anne Thomson. Violin, Royal Liverpool
Philharmonic Orchestra. Photographed with the
Port of Liverpool Building and the Liver Birds
in the background.

The Russian Revolution

The 2005-2006 season was Gerard Schwarz's last as the Liverpool Phil's Music Director. His departure was not without controversy, attracting considerable comment in the local and national press. The job of identifying potential candidates for the post of Principal Conductor fell to a team led by the Society's Chairman, Roger Lewis, Chief Executive, Michael Elliott, and Executive Director, Andrew Cornall, who had joined from the record company Decca and had been responsible for the orchestra's artistic planning since the summer of 2004. Even they would not have been able to predict just how inspired their choice was to prove to be.

In June 2005, Vasily Petrenko was announced as the Royal Liverpool Philharmonic's Principal Conductor. He would take up the role from September, 2006. At 29 years old, he was both the youngest person to have held the position and a virtual unknown. It is easy with hindsight to recognise the wisdom of his appointment but, at the time, handing him the job was an inspired and calculated gamble. The history of symphony orchestras and opera companies the world over is littered with young up-and-coming conductors who do not quite manage to fulfil their potential; come to that, there are plenty of experienced hands who fail to cut the mustard when they are united with a new orchestra on a permanent basis.

Petrenko's Liverpool debut with the Phil in November 2004, and subsequent appearances in October and December 2005, had created huge excitement. The *Daily Telegraph* said it was:

> … memorable for the sheer electricity emanating from the podium. Instantly there was a sense of dialogue between conductor and musicians, between one orchestral family and another, between one phrase and the next, to release natural-seeming eloquence from his players.

Vasily Petrenko

Born: St Petersburg, 1976
Principal Conductor: 2006 onwards

Born and educated in St Petersburg, at the St Petersburg Capella Boys Music School and the St Petersburg Conservatoire, Vasily Petrenko was Resident Conductor at the St Petersburg State Opera and Ballet Theatre from 1994 to 1997 and Chief Conductor of the State Academy Orchestra of St Petersburg from 2004 to 2007.

Recent and future highlights include his BBC Proms debut with the Liverpool Phil and debut with the London Symphony Orchestra, and touring with the European Union Youth Orchestra. He has also conducted the Netherlands Radio Philharmonic, London Philharmonic, the Rotterdam Philharmonic, Leipzig Gewandhausorchester, NHK Symphony and Budapest Festival Orchestras, the Iceland Symphony and the National Youth Orchestra of Great Britain, of which he was appointed Principal Conductor in December 2008.

Following his US debut in the 2007–2008 season, he will make his debuts with the Dallas, Baltimore, Cincinnati, Milwaukee, Honolulu and St Louis Symphonies in 2008–2009. Forthcoming US engagements include the Los Angeles Philharmonic, San Francisco, Atlanta and Chicago Symphonies and the Philadelphia Orchestra. With a wide opera repertoire, he has conducted three productions in recent seasons at the Netherlands Reisopera. Future plans include his debuts at Glyndebourne Festival Opera and the Opera de Paris.

Petrenko was Gramophone Young Artist of the Year 2007, and was named Personality of the Year at the 2008 Liverpool Scouseology Awards. Recordings with the Royal Liverpool Philharmonic include a double bill of Fleishman's *Rothschild's Violin* and Shostakovich's *The Gamblers*, suites from Tchaikovsky's ballets and Tchaikovsky's *Manfred Symphony*. Future recording projects with the Phil include the Shostakovich symphony cycle and Rachmaninov's orchestral music.

A football aficionado, he is a supporter of Zenit St Petersburg, and takes a keen interest in Merseyside's three clubs, Liverpool, Everton and Tranmere Rovers. When in England, he lives on Wirral with his wife and son.

Petrenko's arrival on Merseyside was heralded with a major advertising campaign. Billboards bearing the legend 'Liverpool's latest signing' and a huge picture of the young Russian maestro sprang up all over the area. No doubt, the marketing created interest – the Phil's new conductor was young and photogenic – but it was on the platform that the proof of the wisdom of his signing became clear.

Rarely can the arrival of one individual have galvanized an artistic organisation to so great an extent. London-based critics began to reassess their preconceptions about the Royal Liverpool Philharmonic. There was a palpable sense that this was an orchestra and a conductor that was going places. Tim Ashley wrote in *The Guardian*:

> Petrenko's impact has been tremendous. There is now a crackle of electricity whenever you hear the Phil play … he is a remarkable artist, turning in startling performances of the broadest of repertoires.

Petrenko himself told Geoffrey Norris of the *Daily Telegraph*:

> One point that I really appreciate in the musicians is their willingness to work. From the first moment I arrived, I felt they were hungry for rehearsals and to improve themselves. I think there was probably enthusiasm before, but I bring my own ideas that most of the musicians share with me, so there is that possibility of going together in the same direction.

Just six months after Petrenko's arrival, his three-year contract was extended for a further three-year period, meaning that he will continue to direct the orchestra until at least 2012. Ticket sales for his concerts started to boom and there were clear indications that he was bringing a new younger audience to the Phil. What appeared to be challenging box office targets at the beginning of the 2006-2007 season were comfortably met three months ahead of schedule. The same season had seen James Clark and Thelma Handy being appointed as Joint Leaders of the orchestra.

In October 2007, Petrenko was named 'Young Artist of the Year' at the Classic FM Gramophone Awards, among the most prestigious accolades in classical music. The judges made special reference to his debut CD release with the RLPO. The CD, recorded live in concert at the Philharmonic Hall, featured singers from the

A packed Philharmonic Hall, an increasingly common sight today.

The billboard campaign announcing Vasily Petrenko's arrival in Liverpool.

Liverpool's Latest Signing

Vasily Petrenko, Principal Conductor

Royal Liverpool Philharmonic Orchestra

CLASSIC *f*M

Orchestra in North West England

www.liverpoolphil.com

The Royal Liverpool
Philharmonic Orchestra in the
virtual world of Second Life.

A scene from the European
Opera Centre's production of
Shostakovich's *The Gamblers*,
with the RLPO conducted by
Vasily Petrenko.

European Opera Centre and included two lesser-known works: Shostakovich's *The Gamblers* and Fleishman's *Rothschild's Violin.* It was chosen as the Editor's Choice in *The Gramophone* in June 2007. The Editor, James Inverne, wrote:

> Vasily Petrenko has not been long on Merseyside, but already he is emerging as one of Liverpool's musical heroes ... A set to buy, a maestro to watch.

At the same ceremony, the Liverpool Phil was also given an award for its innovative use of the internet to reach out to new audiences, through the online 'Second Life' community. In a world first, brokered by the Phil's Executive Director of Marketing, Millicent Jones, one hundred virtual guests from around the world, represented by their avatars, joined the regular concert-goers who took their seats in the Philharmonic Hall. They 'sat' in a 3D virtual version of the hall, simultaneously watching and listening live as the real orchestra performed in Liverpool, conducted by Vasily Petrenko. They were joined by many more of the nine million residents of Second Life across the world, who watched the performance broadcast live, courtesy of Second Life's own cable TV network. A recorded version of the broadcast was then available to Second Life residents for the next two months.

The initiative attracted global media and public interest. Richard Morrison, the Chief Music Critic for *The Times,* wrote:

> ... the intrepid Royal Liverpool Philharmonic has taken this brave plunge into cyberspatial concert giving ... Second Life would seem one way for orchestras to disseminate their music-making on a massively enhanced scale without budging from the concert hall.

2008 European Capital of Culture

Vasily Petrenko, the Royal Liverpool Philharmonic Orchestra and Philharmonic Hall were at the centre of Liverpool's celebrations as European Capital of Culture in 2008. And there is little doubt that Petrenko emerged as one of the real stars of the year and that the reputation of the Liverpool Phil was greatly enhanced by the celebrations.

Petrenko conducted the Capital of Culture's official opening event, *Liverpool: The Musical*, at the brand new *Liverpool Echo* Arena. The orchestra sat at the back of the Arena's massive stage in a vertical grid of cubes, stacked floor-to-ceiling on top of each other. It was a visually arresting site with Petrenko conducting the soundtrack to the evening from a scissor lift.

In her review of the concert on the *Liverpool Confidential* website, Angie Sammons wrote:

> Liverpool got there, with a little help from its friends, but it was one less obvious friend who clinched it … a Russian who now, surely, must be recognised as the City's most valuable treasure … Vasily Petrenko was whizzed into the sky aboard a steel platform to conduct the RLPO. The City is extremely lucky to have a world class orchestra at its disposal, and this opener was stunning in its acoustics, in its spectacle and in its ambition.

The orchestra delivered a formidable artistic programme for the year, which included no fewer than thirty new music commissions, including major works from Sir John Tavener and Karl Jenkins, alongside works by Liverpool-born composers John McCabe, Kenneth Hesketh and the BBC Young Musician and Composer of the Year, Mark Simpson. The artists' roll-call included Sir Simon Rattle and Vladimir Ashkenazy, both of whom took the title Artist Laureate 2008. Other visiting stars included Bryn Terfel, Midori, Yuri Bashmet, Ian Bostridge, Janine Jansen, Wayne Shorter and Sir Charles Mackerras, who has a rich heritage of conducting the Liverpool Phil over many years. He was named the RLPO's Conductor Emeritus at the beginning of 2009, succeeding Vernon Handley CBE, who had held this honorary position from 1997 until his death in September 2008.

During 2008, Petrenko took the orchestra to London for three visits to the Royal Albert Hall – twice for Classic FM Live concerts and once to make his BBC Proms debut. There was also a tour to the Prague Autumn Festival and to Holland and Germany and a series of out-of-town British dates that included Newcastle, Carlisle, Huddersfield, Derby, the North Wales International Festival, Preston and Blackburn. Petrenko and the Liverpool Phil have become a hot ticket. Right now, it seems that

The world première of Sir John Tavener's *Requiem* at the Liverpool Metropolitan Cathedral, 28th February 2008.

everybody wants to hear this dynamic new partnership for themselves.

Both during 2008 itself, and in the run-up to the year, the Royal Liverpool Philharmonic was a central contributor to the organisation of the European Capital of Culture year. All eight of the major cultural organisations in the City worked closely together and this has been recognised by the creation of the Liverpool Arts Regeneration Consortium. The group has been awarded project funding from Arts Council England and the Liverpool Phil is its managing partner.

The Future

With the 2008 Capital of Culture year now over, and with 'the Petrenko effect' showing every sign of growing rather than waning, the Royal Liverpool Philharmonic is enjoying a glorious period in its history, to rival those of Sir Malcolm Sargent, Sir John Pritchard and Sir Charles Groves. Without doubt, it is in better shape than it has been at any time in the past thirty years, and perhaps for much longer. Petrenko's reign has the potential to sit at the summit of the Phil's achievements. Only time will tell, but parallels are already being drawn to the tenure of that other Liverpool Legend, Sir Simon Rattle, at the City of Birmingham Symphony Orchestra. The people of Liverpool have taken their new maestro to their hearts, naming him International Scouser of the Year at the City's annual Scouseology Awards.

The Liverpool Phil has the stability of knowing that its dynamic young conductor will remain with the orchestra until at least the end of the 2012 season. The pathway to making music on Merseyside has never been an easy one and who knows what unexpected problems the Royal Liverpool Philharmonic will have to face in the coming years; certainly, funding remains a perpetual concern, but the orchestra's management has successfully negotiated that jungle over recent years. So long as there are no dramatic changes in the funding policies of Arts Council England or of Liverpool City Council, then the Royal Liverpool Philharmonic should be able to continue to build on the solid foundations laid since the organisation went through the Stabilisation process in the past few years. It is now entering a new era, after the appointment of the Liverpool Phil's Chief Executive, Michael Elliott, as the Director of Culture at the Department of Culture Media & Sport. His replacement as Chief Executive is Michael Eakin, the former Chief Executive of Arts Council England in the North West. Together with the chairman, Lorraine Rogers, who is also Chief Executive of the Mersey Partnership, Eakin's background must make him uniquely qualified to lead the Liverpool Phil through the funding maze.

Rather than looking wistfully at the great successes of the past, the Royal Liverpool Philharmonic is now an organisation that is looking forward to a glorious future. Plans are already afoot to examine ways of developing the area surrounding the Philharmonic Hall, to provide on-site rehearsal and recital spaces, practice and music workshop rooms, as well as new front-of-house and retail areas. Meanwhile, *Liverpool Phil at the Friary* is now fully operational as a rehearsal and recording space.

Throughout all of the years of the Phil's existence, there has been one common core running through the organisation's history: the desire to present the greatest music to the people of Liverpool. And, since 1840, the Phil has provided an uninterrupted soundtrack to local, national and international events.

In the end, the Liverpool Phil has always been the Liverpool Phil because of the music – and the musicians that make it. Whatever else was going on in the City, the country, or the world ... the Royal Liverpool Philharmonic, the band that created the original Liverpool Sound, always played on.

Liverpool Phil at the Friary.

The Phil's 2008

Liverpool's tenure as European Capital of Culture 2008 was a memorable one. The Liverpool Phil's contribution to the special year was heralded in all quarters for its excellence, innovation, participation and excitement.

"Almost no large scale Culture year event was complete without the ubiquitious presence of of Vasily Petrenko and the Royal Liverpool Philharmonic Orchestra. From the Viennese Balls to the Tavener and Verdi Requiems and their appearance at the BBC Proms, the Phil provided the soundtrack to the year." *Liverpool Daily Post*

On the following pages are some of the highlights of the Liverpool Phil's 2008.

Classic FM in Liverpool. Liverpool's tallest building, the Beetham Organisation's West Tower, hosted the Liverpool Phil's media partner, Classic FM on 3rd January, when the station relocated from its home in London's West End for the first time in its fifteen-year history, to broadcast live from Liverpool for 24 hours, marking the start of European Capital of Culture year.

Holocaust Memorial Day Commemoration Event, 27th January at Liverpool Philharmonic Hall. The Archbishop of Canterbury, Dr Rowan Williams, Britain's Chief Rabbi, Sir Jonathan Sacks, His Excellency the Ambassador of the State of Israel, Ron Prosor, and the Secretary of State for Communities, Hazel Blears, were among many dignitaries, civic leaders and guests from across the UK who attended the event at Philharmonic Hall. Afterwards, hundreds of people signed their own pledge against genocide on a giant banner lying along Hope Street, which bore the words of the seven Stockholm Commitments against racism and genocide.

Liverpool Phil on the Record. The Royal Liverpool Philharmonic archive was unveiled to the general public for the first time in 2008, at a special event at the Picton Library Liverpool. The archive, now held at Liverpool Record Office, took a full-time archivist and 30 volunteers two years to catalogue. The project was initiated by amateur archivist, the late Vin Tyndall, who had dedicated over twenty years of his life to voluntarily collating much of the archive.

Fresh Festival, Liverpool Philharmonic Hall and venues around Hope Street. The Bays/Heritage Orchestra.

Legendary jazz saxophonist Wayne Shorter and his quartet perform with the Liverpool Phil, conducted by Clark Rundell. "For sheer audacity in mounting this ambitious venture, Fresh Festival deserves huge praise." *The Guardian*.

Viennese Balls, St George's Hall, Liverpool. Hundreds of waltzing feet were serenaded by the music of the Strauss waltz kings, played by the Royal Liverpool Philharmonic Orchestra conducted by Vasily Petrenko, with the dancing led by Strictly Come Dancing stars, Anton du Beke and Erin Boag. The Viennese Balls marked the beginning of a city-wide Viennese theme inspired by the Gustav Klimt exhibition at Tate Liverpool.

BBC Electric Proms, Liverpool Philharmonic Hall. Razorlight (pictured) and the Last Shadow Puppets played at the Hall during a pulsating weekend of music when Liverpool co-hosted this unique festival with London, which included live broadcasts on BBC radio and TV.

Northern Charity Première. Paul McCartney's *Ecce Cor Meum* (*Behold My Heart*). 1st May 2008, Liverpool Cathedral. Sir Paul is pictured here during rehearsals.

World Première, Karl Jenkins *Stabat Mater*, Liverpool Cathedral. "Jenkins himself, conducting the RLPO, scores full marks for being an approachable composer … witness the full house, the standing ovation and the fact that people had travelled miles to hear the piece. There were moments of extreme, soul-searching beauty." *Liverpool Daily Post*.

An Evening with Bryn Terfel, Liverpool Philharmonic Hall. "Expectations were high that the world-class baritone's first-ever collaboration with Liverpool's latest classical darling, Vasily Petrenko would light a few fires. Few could have predicted just how spectacular a success it would be." *Liverpool Daily Post*.

Liverpool Arabic Arts Festival –
Khaled, Liverpool Philharmonic
Hall. "He's a musical phenomenon
in the Arab world and a superstar
across many areas of the globe.
Khaled produced a string of
pulsating hits, with the audience
spilling out on to Hope Street to
continue the party." *Liverpool Echo*.

Ensemble 10/10 Late at Tate
Liverpool. The Phil's new music
group gave several recitals at Tate
Liverpool, providing a musical
upbeat to the Gustav Klimt
exhibition on display during 2008.

Opposite. Elvis Costello with the
RLPO, Liverpool Philharmonic Hall.
"And the highlights kept coming –
through them all, the Phil crackled
and fizzed with life and energy.
'That's the Capital of Culture right
there!' Elvis exclaimed, pointing
behind him to the trendily black-
clad orchestra after one especially
blistering crescendo." *Liverpool
Confidential*.

226

Britten's *War Requiem*, Liverpool Cathedral. "For if the *War Requiem* is neither easy to perform nor to hear, it is staggeringly difficult to stage, and to pack a cathedral the size of Gilbert Scott's masterpiece with an eager, appreciative audience and choral and orchestral forces from the City and its twin, Cologne, was a triumph." *The Observer*.

Summer Classics. "On a balmy night at the seaside in Southport Victoria Park, a fizzing Phil gave a majestic parade through Proms favourites" *Liverpool Echo*.

BBC Proms 2008, Royal Albert Hall, London. Vasily Petrenko made his BBC Proms debut with the RLPO on 1st August 2008. The sold-out and critically acclaimed concert included Rachmaninov's *Symphonic Dances*; the world première of *Graven Image*, a joint BBC / Liverpool Phil commission by Composer in the House, Kenneth Hesketh; and the internationally acclaimed young pianist, Liverpudlian Paul Lewis, playing Beethoven's Fourth Piano Concerto.

On 22nd May, the Phil welcomed our Patron, Her Majesty the Queen, as part of her visit to Liverpool during 2008. Her Majesty enjoyed a performance by the RLPO, conducted by Sir Andrew Davis. Eight-year-old Liverpool Philharmonic Youth Choir member Anishna Sunil and cellist Ian Bracken presented a bouquet and a Liverpool Phil concert programme published in the Queen's coronation year, 1953.

Amateur musicians of all ages joined musicians of the Royal Liverpool Philharmonic Orchestra to form Superorchestra, rehearsing and then performing music by Mozart, Tchaikovsky, Orff, Parry and Tavener at Liverpool Philharmonic Hall.

Opposite. Hope Street Feast. Over 10,000 people enjoyed a day of sunshine, free music, dance, theatre, art and food, including an open day at Philharmonic Hall.

Sir Simon Rattle returned to Philharmonic Hall where he began his career for two eagerly anticipated concerts in 2008: first with the Berliner Philharmoniker, and later in the year to conduct the Royal Liverpool Philharmonic Orchestra (pictured here). The concert included the world première of a new work by Brett Dean, *Songs of Joy*.

Sir Simon led a masterclass with Liverpool Philharmonic Youth Orchestra, of which he is Patron. He joined the Youth Orchestra (formerly known as Merseyside Youth Orchestra) as a percussionist, aged ten.

The Rightful Owners of the Song, Liverpool Philharmonic Hall. The culmination of a year-long project devised by musician Jonathan Raisin celebrated Liverpool's tradition of pub-singing in a concert with the RLPO pictured here with singer Tony Peters.

John Lennon Songbook, Liverpool Philharmonic Hall. "The Phil has been at the fulcrum of some of the greatest musical moments of Capital of Culture year so far, most especially in its forays away from the purely classical and into the world of pop. Arguably the best of all came last Friday night with the reworking of the Lennon songbook, the official 08 musical tribute to the renegade Beatle and the second of a sell-out performance featuring local lad Mark McGann and acclaimed jazz-influenced vocalists Curtis Stigers and Claire Martin." *Liverpool Daily Post*.

Verdi Requiem, Liverpool Metropolitan Cathedral. Vasily Petrenko conducted the Royal Liverpool Philharmonic Orchestra and Choir, joined by Huddersfield Choral Society and Leeds Philharmonic Society and a star-studded cast of international soloists, making Verdi's choral extravaganza a night to remember.

Recording at the Phil. The Phil's in-house recording team, Merseysound's Dave Pigott and Mike Ogonovsky, discuss a latest RLPO recording with Vasily Petrenko.

In 2009, Sir Charles Mackerras, pictured rehearsing with the Phil, was appointed Conductor Emeritus, succeeding the late Vernon Handley CBE who had held the honorary position from 1997 to 2008.

ROYAL LIVERPOOL PHILHARMONIC PRINCIPAL CONDUCTORS

1840	John Russell, Thomas Clough
1841	Thomas Clough, William Sudlow
1842	William Sudlow
1843	J Zeugheer Herrmann
1865	Alfred Mellon
1867	Sir Julius Benedict
1880	Max Bruch
1883	Sir Charles Hallé
1895	Sir Frederic Cowen
1913	Guest Conductors, including Sir Thomas Beecham, Sir Henry Wood, Sir Hamilton Harty
1942	Sir Malcolm Sargent
1948	Hugo Rignold
1954	Sir John Pritchard and Guests
1955	Efrem Kurtz and Sir John Pritchard
1957	Sir John Pritchard
1963	Sir Charles Groves
1977	Walter Weller
1980	David Atherton
1983	Marek Janowski
1987	Libor Pešek KBE
1997	Petr Altrichter
2001	Gerard Schwarz
2006	Vasily Petrenko

ROYAL LIVERPOOL PHILHARMONIC CHORUS MASTERS

1883	Horatio Arthur Branscombe
1913	Harry Evans (Resident Choral Conductor)
1914	RH Wilson
1917	Alfred Benton
1918	Dr Arthur W Pollitt
1929	Dr JE Wallace
1941	John Tobin (Choral Conductor)
1947	Dr JE Wallace
1970	Edmund Walters
1985	Professor Ian Tracey

ROYAL LIVERPOOL PHILHARMONIC ORCHESTRA LEADERS

1845	HF Aldridge
1849	EW Thomas
1883	Ludwig Straus
1889	Willy Hess
1895	Adolph Brodsky
1896	Risegari
1899	Arthur W Payne
1905	C Rawdon Briggs
1913	Arthur Catterall
1929	Alfred Barker
1939	Thomas Matthews
1940	Henry Holst
1945	David Wise
1947	Manoug Parikian
1948	Henry Datyner
1955	Peter Mountain
1966	Paul Collins
1966	Clifford Knowles
1973	Alan Traverse
1979	Malcolm Stewart
2006	James Clark and Thelma Handy

ROYAL LIVERPOOL PHILHARMONIC SECRETARIES / CHIEF EXECUTIVES

1840	William Sudlow
1855	Henry Sudlow
1884	G Broadbent
1909	WJ Riley
1939	WR Fell
1945	AJ Beard
1946	WC Stiff
1956	Gerald McDonald
1964	Stephen Gray
1987	David Pratley
1988	Anthony Woodcock
1991	Robert Creech
1993	Antony Lewis-Crosby
2001	Michael Elliott
2008	Michael Eakin

ROYAL LIVERPOOL PHILHARMONIC CHAIRMEN

1840	RW Bateson	1894	Walter H Wilson	1948	Thomas Pennycuick
1842	William Clare	1895	Elisha Smith	1949	Alderman Luke Hogan
1843	John B Brancker	1896	Walter C Clark	1950	Professor Lyon Blease
1849	John H Turner	1897	John Wilson	1951	Alderman David J Lewis
1851	The Earl of Sefton	1898	Theodore Von Sobbe	1955	Alderman Harry Livermore
1852	Alfred Castellain	1899	Walter H Wilson	1958	Alderman John Braddock
1853	Benjamin H Jones	1900	Andrew L Coltart	1959	Alderman Harry Livermore
1854	Hardman Earle	1901	Lieutenant-Colonel Thomas Gee	1961	Alderman Patrick Rathbone
1856	HW Meade King			1963	Alderman Harry Livermore
1857	WH Maclean	1902	Thomas C Ryley	1967	Andrew McKie Ried
1858	William Langton	1903	Theodore Von Sobbe	1971	Kenneth Stern
1859	PG Heyworth	1904	Andrew L Coltart	1972	Sir Harry Livermore
1860	Courtenay Cruttenden	1905	Colonel Thomas Gee	1974	Councillor Ben Shaw
1861	John Brancker	1906	TE Paget	1977	Councillor John Last
1862	AG Kurtz	1907	Sir WB Bowring, Bart	1981	Councillor Ben Shaw
1864	P Vance	1908	Eustace Carey	1984	Councillor Jim Riley
1865	JN Stolterfoht	1909	TE Paget	1986	Councillor John Last
1866	James Lister	1910	WE Willink	1987	Councillor Jim Riley
1867	HF Hornby	1911	Richard Caton	1988	John Last
1868	W Winter Raffles	1912	George Nicholson	1992	Brian Thaxter
1869	Laurence R Baily	1913	JG Earle	1996	Peter Johnson
1870	Robert J King	1914	WE Willink	2000	Peter Toyne
1871	Frederic H Boult	1915	Henry E Rensburg	2003	Roger Lewis
1872	John Brancker	1916	Captain Mark P Rathbone	2006	Lorraine Rogers
1874	JJ Drysdale	1917	Edward A Behrend		
1875	TE Paget	1918	WE Willink		
1876	Laurence R Baily	1919	John H Kenion		
1877	Stewart H Brown	1920	Colonel Henry Wainwright		
1878	PF Garnett	1921	Major Mark P Rathbone		
1879	Holbrook Gaskell	1922	J Middlemass Hunt		
1880	Alfred Turner	1923	Arthur A Mussen		
1881	J Marke Wood	1924	George Brocklehurst		
1882	Alfred Castellain	1925	H Milner Brown		
1883	George R Cox	1926	Ainslie J Robertson		
1885	W Newall Watson	1927	John D Hayward		
1886	TE Paget	1928	Sir Arnold Rushton		
1887	Richard Hobson	1929	Edward A Behrend		
1888	Walter C Clark	1930	HA Thew		
1889	Colonel Thomas Wilson	1931	W Ernest Taylor		
1890	TE Paget	1932	George R Norris		
1891	Theodore Von Sobbe	1933	Edward A Behrend		
1892	John Wilson	1934	Ainslie J Robertson		
		1936	Professor Walter J Dilling		
		1940	Sir David L Webster		
		1946	Professor Walter J Dilling		

RLPO Première Performances

Date	Composer	Work	Type
27 August 1849	GA MacFarren	Scene and Aria 'Andromaca'	World
27 August 1849	Julius Benedict	Festival Overture	World
30 April 1850	E Biletta	Song and Chrous, 'Fill me a goblet of bright champagne'	World
16 August 1850	Vivier	Andante for solo horn	World
16 August 1850	Vivier	Chase for solo horn	World
12 November 1850	Charles Edward Horsley	David, a sacred oratorio	World
18 April 1854	Henry Tivendell	Overture, Aladdin	World
21 April 1857	S Percival	The Lyre, a cantata for four voices, chorus and orchestra	World
7 January 1862	Gioachino Rossini	Duo 'Bolero'	World
14 April 1863	Goldberg	Aria 'La Costanza'	World
21 February 1865	Julius Benedict	Duet, 'Why am I not thy guardian, dear'	World
8 December 1866	Lindsay Sloper	Ballad Fantasia on Airs	World
18 January 1868	Enrico Bevignani	'Godiamo'	World
28 January 1868	Enrico Bevignani	Ballad, 'A knight came to impart'	World
9 May 1868	W Ganz	Song, 'Forget Me Not'	World
9 May 1868	W Ganz	Song, 'The Faithful Echo'	World
12 January 1869	EW Thomas	Barcarolle and Tarantella for solo violin	World
9 February 1869	Carl Eckert	Konzert-Stück	UK
1 February 1870	CFE Horneman	Overture, Aladdin	UK
8 January 1878	Joachim Raff	Violin Concerto	World
4 November 1879	Carl Reinthaler	Symphony in D, Op.12	UK
16 December 1879	Charles E Stephens	A Recollection of the Past	World
31 March 1880	John Thomas	Adagio, Harp	World
2 November 1880	Max Bruch	Hebrew Melodies	World
22 February 1881	Max Bruch	Fantasia, Op.46	UK
7 February 1882	Max Bruch	Kol Nidrei	World
5 February 1889	Sir Alexander Campbell Mackenzie	The Dream of Jubal	World
2 April 1889	Sir Frederic Cowen	Ruth	World
30 March 1897	Hector Berlioz	Les Troyens	UK
26 October 1909	Friedrich Gernsheim	Cello Concerto in E minor, Op.78	UK
15 December 1914	Gabriel Pierné	The Children's Crusade	UK
5 December 1916	Granville Bantock	Hebridean Symphony	English
17 November 1917	Ernest Bryson	The Stranger for baritone solo, chorus and orchestra	World
30 November 1918	Eugene Goossens	Four Conceits, for orchestra, Op.20	World
15 March 1921	Sergei Rachmaninov	The Bells	UK
20 March 1928	Ladislav Vycpálek	Cantata, The Last Things of Man	UK
11 March 1930	Sergei Rachmaninov	Three Russian Songs, Op.41	UK

13 October 1936	Arnold Bax	Overture, Rogue's Comedy	World
10 October 1945	Sir Michael Tippett	Symphony No.1	World
20 October 1945	Béla Bartók	Concerto for Orchestra	UK
19 January 1946	EJ Moeran	Violin Concerto	UK
15 October 1946	Benjamin Britten	Young Person's Guide to the Orchestra	World
27 September 1949	Sergei Prokofiev	Ballet Suite from 'Cinderella'	UK
17 January 1950	Benjamin Frankel	Overture, Mayday	World
10 October 1951	Jean Martinon	Sinfoniette for Strings, Harp, Piano and Timpani	UK
18 December 1951	Paul Hindemith	Piano Concerto	UK
29 January 1952	Karl Rankl	Symphony No.1	UK
30 January 1952	Bohuslav Martinů	Violin Concerto	UK
25 March 1952	Marcel Mihalovici	Toccata for Piano and Orchestra	UK
6 October 1953	Sir Michael Tippett	Ritual Dances	UK
20 September 1955	Otmar Nussio	Dances of Majorca	UK
4 October 1955	Malcolm Lipkin	Tragic Overture	World
13 November 1956	Sir William Walton	Johannesburg Festival Overture	UK
2 December 1957	Sir Malcolm Arnold	Symphony No.3	World
22 September 1958	Iain Hamilton	Sonata for Chamber Orchestra	World
20 October 1958	Humphrey Searle	Symphony No.2	World
18 January 1960	Harry Somers	Passacaglia and Fugue	World
18 January 1960	Karl-Birger Blomdahl	Concerto for Piano and Wind	UK
22 February 1960	Roger Sessions	Violin Concerto	UK
2 May 1960	Don Banks	Four Orchestral Pieces	UK
2 May 1960	Hans Werner Henze	Quattro Poemi	UK
2 May 1960	Gunther Schuller	Dramatic Overture	UK
2 September 1960	Sir William Walton	Symphony No.2	UK
3 September 1960	Humphrey Searle	Symphony No.3	World
24 October 1960	Sir Peter Maxwell Davies	Prolation	UK
9 October 1961	Alexander Goehr	Sutter's Gold	World
24 November 1961	Sir William Walton	Gloria	World
18 January 1966	Malcolm Lipkin	Sinfonia Roma	World
29 March 1966	William Mathias	Concerto for Orchestra	World
17 October 1967	Kenneth Leighton	Symphony	UK
17 September 1968	Gordon Crosse	'For the Unfallen' for Tenor, Horn and Strings	World
1 April 1969	John McCabe	Harpsichord Concerto	World
29 April 1969	Witold Lutoslawski	Symphony No.2	UK
16 September 1969	Alberto Ginastera	Violin Concerto	UK
30 September 1969	Roger Smalley	Gloria Tibi Trinitatis I	World
25 November 1969	Benjamin Frankel	Symphony No.6	World
28 June 1970	Sir William Walton	Improvisations on an Impromptu by Benjamin Britten	World
19 September 1970	Grażyha Bacewicz	Viola Concerto	UK
5 January 1971	Edmund Rubbra	Symphony No.8	World

5 January 1971	Patrick Standford	Preludio Ostinato	World
14 September 1971	Dmitri Shostakovich	Symphony No.13	Western Europe
7 December 1971	Benjamin Frankel	Symphony No.8	World
19 February 1972	John McCabe	Metamorphoses for harpsichord and orchestra	World
19 September 1972	Hugh Wood	Violin Concerto	World
20 February 1973	Edmund Rubbra	Symphony No.9	World
1 October 1974	Lief Segerstam	Pandora Sketches	UK
23 October 1974	Wilfred Josephs	Night Music	World
12 November 1974	Aulis Sallinen	Symphonic Dialogue for Percussion and Orchestra	UK
3 February 1976	Giles Swayne	Orlando's Music	World
30 November 1976	Luciano Berio	La Ritirata Notturna di Madrid	UK
18 January 1977	Graham Whettam	Sinfonia Intrepida	World
16 April 1977	Dmitri Shostakovich	Suite on Poems of Michelangelo for bass and orchestra	UK
5 August 1977	John McCabe	Piano Concerto No.3 'Dialogues'	World
25 November 1978	HK Gruber	Frankenstein!! (Chanson Cycle for baritone voice and orchestra)	World
18 March 1980	Stephen Pratt	Some of their Number for orchestra	World
10 January 1981	Michael Berkeley	Flames	World
2 February 1982	Edward Cowie	Concerto for Orchestra	World
2 March 1982	Eric Wolfgang Korngold	Symphony in F sharp	UK
14 May 1983	William Mathias	Symphony No.2	World
1 February 1984	Edward Cowie	Symphony No.1 (American)	World
3 October 1984	Robert Simpson	Symphony No.7	World
30 November 1985	Lukas Foss	Night Music for John Lennon for brass quintet and orchestra	UK
23 April 1986	Geoffrey Poole	Visions	First Public Performance
4 October 1986	Steve Reich	Variations for Winds, Strings and Keyboards	UK
26 November 1986	Robert Simpson	Nielsen Variations	World
25 November 1987	Glyn Perrin	Tu, même	World
24 January 1989	Aaron Copland	Jubilee Variation	UK
4 February 1989	John Adams	The Chairman Dances	UK
4 February 1989	Tōru Takemitsu	Gitimalya	UK
20 September 1989	Alfred Schnittke	Concerto Grosso No.4 / Symphony No.5	UK
16 May 1990	James Wishart	Oran Hiortach (St Kilda Song)	World
16 January 1991	Robert Simpson	Symphony No.10	World
18 May 1991	Stephen Pratt	Uneasy Vespers (Part 1)	World
28 June 1991	Sir Paul McCartney / Carl Davis	Liverpool Oratorio	World
16 October 1991	Anthony Powers	Horn Concerto	World
8 January 1993	Judith Weir	Music, Untangled	UK
14 September 1995	Graham Fitkin	Fanfare	World
23 September 1995	Alfred Schnittke	For Liverpool	World
20 March 1996	Philip Glass	Concerto for Saxophone Quartet	UK
27 April 1996	Richard Gordon-Smith	Lowlands Away	World
10 February 1999	Gary Carpenter	Satie – Variations for Orchestra	World

15 May 1999	Wojciech Kilar	Krzesany	UK
20 October 1999	Adam Gorb	Clarinet Concerto	World
21 February 2001	David Horne	The Year's Midnight	World
16 September 2001	Gustav Mahler, arr Alexander Asteriades	Piano Quartet in A minor arranged for strings	European
4 May 2002	Daniel Brewbaker	Fields of Vision	European
9 January 2003	Behzad Ranjbaran	Violin Concerto	World
30 October 2003	Stephen Pratt	Violin Concerto	World
22 May 2004	David Horne	Concerto for Orchestra	World
20 October 2005	Tom Moss	Rhapsody Revisited	World
28 December 2005	Dmitri Shostakovich	The Silly Little Mouse (with specially-written words by David Conolly and Hannah Davis)	World
25 February 2006	Ross Edwards	Bird Spirit Dreaming (oboe concerto)	UK
20 May 2006	Ludovico Einaudi	Divenire (for solo piano, cello, strings and harp)	World
28 October 2006	Joby Talbot	Desolation Wilderness (trumpet concerto)	World
18 November 2006	Carl Davis	Cyrano: 'The Cadets of Gascoyne: Rataplan'	World
25 November 2006	Louis Andriessen, arr. Clark Rundell	Vermeer Pictures	UK
7 December 2006	Christian Lindberg	Mandrake in the Corner	UK
7 January 2007	Harold Arlen, EY Yarburg & Herbert Stothart	The Wizard of Oz with Live Music	UK première of the film with live music
17 March 2007	Stephen Hough	The Loneliest Wilderness (Elegy for Cello and Orchestra)	World
7 June 2007	Haim Permont	Oboe Concerto	World
14 September 2007	Kenneth Hesketh	A Rhyme for the Season	World
14 September 2007	John McCabe	Symphony 'Labyrinth'	World
20 October 2007	Jon Lord	Durham Concerto	World
6 December 2007	Emily Howard	Magnetite	World
6 December 2007	Ludwig van Beethoven, orch. Gustav Mahler	Symphony No.9 'Choral'	World
19 January 2008	Felix Mendelssohn	Piano Concerto No.3	UK première of the reconstruction by Marcello Bufalini
19 January 2008	Kenneth Hesketh	Like the sea, like time	World
26 February 2008	Sir John Tavener	Requiem	World
15 March 2008	Karl Jenkins	Stabat Mater	World
5 April 2008	Michael Nyman	gdm for marimba and orchestra	UK
14 June 2008	Richard Strauss	Der Rosenkavalier – Live music with the 1926 silent film	UK première of the live music with the 1926 silent film, as reconstructed by European Film Philharmonic
25 July 2008	John Harle	Earthlight	World
1 August 2008	Kenneth Hesketh	Graven Image	World
2 October 2008	Brett Dean	Songs of Joy	World
11 October 2008	Mark Simpson	A Mirror-Fragment	World
23 October 2008	Stephen Pratt	Uneasy Vespers (Part II)	World

Ensemble 10/10 Première Performances

Date	Composer	Title	
30 May 1998	Ian Gardiner	Sad Cadences	World
23 March 1999	Carlos Chavez	Energia	UK
23 March 1999	Joseph Schwantner	Distant Runes and Incantations	European
23 March 1999	Stephen Albert	Flower of the Mountain	UK
23 March 1999	Christopher Rouse	Compline	European
23 March 1999	Aaron Jay Kernis	Simple Songs	European
1 May 1999	Naoki Kita	Sunspot	World
1 May 1999	Paul Stroud	'A Fear of Dist'	World
27 May 2000	David Charles Martin	We do not dream in words	World
27 May 2000	Roddie Skeaping	Five Musical Maquettes	World
27 May 2000	Geoffrey Palmer	Silent Conversation	World
14 December 2000	Gary Carpenter	Flea Circus	World
May 2003	David Horne	Disembodied Instruments	World
May 2003	Stephen Pratt	Lovebytes	World
2 December 2004	Gary Carpenter	Distanza	World
2 December 2004	Ian Gardiner	Toccata, Canzona, Ricercare	World
12 February 2005	Mark Simpson	it was as if the world stood still	World
5 October 2005	Emily Howard	Dualities	World
5 October 2005	Simon Bainbridge	Voiles	World
2 December 2005	Mark Simpson	Septet	World
7 November 2006	Stephen Pratt	Double Act	World
12 November 2006	Richard Barrett	Melos	World
12 November 2006	Olga Neuwirth	torsion: transparent variation	UK

12 November 2006	Robin Hartwell	Unequal Division	World
19 January 2007	Michael Walsh	First Impressions	World
19 January 2007	Kurt Schwertsik	The Longest Ten Minutes	World
19 January 2007	David Horne	Phantom Instruments	World
16 February 2007	Ian Gardiner	Vormittagsspuk (Ghosts before Breakfast)	World
16 February 2007	Ian Gardiner	Rose Hobart	World
16 February 2007	Kenneth Hesketh	Ein Lichtspiel	World
18 March 2007	Gary Carpenter	Sonatinas for Alto Saxophone and Chamber Orchestra	World
18 March 2007	Ian Stephens	… through the affrighted air …	World
10 May 2007	Howard Skempton	Piazza	World
10 May 2007	Ian Gardiner	L'escalier en spirale	World
3 October 2007	Graham Fitkin	Subterfuge for cello and ensemble	World
3 October 2007	Steve Martland	Reveille	World
16 January 2008	Kate Threlfall, arr. Clark Rundell	Sunshine, Learn to Love	World première of these arrangements
16 January 2008	Michael Torke	Tropical	World
16 January 2008	Ian Gardiner	listen … move … dance	World
14 May 2008	Mark Simpson	Nur Musik for oboe and ensemble	World
14 May 2008	Lukas Ligeti	Castle of Turns	UK
11 June 2008	James Wishart	The Punishment of Lust	World
8 October 2008	Gary Carpenter	Closing Time for tenor and ensemble	World
8 October 2008	John Casken	The Dream of the Rood	World
19 November 2008	Kenneth Hesketh	Wunderkammer(konzert)	World
19 November 2008	Philip Venables	Anima	World
19 November 2008	Elizabeth Winters	The Silken Thread	World
24 January 2009	Ian Stephens	Oxbow for dai-hu and ensemble	World
6 March 2009	Thomas Davey	Three Movements for oboe and small ensemble	World
6 March 2009	Matthew Sergeant	three visions in a grove of trees	World
6 March 2009	Gemma Wild	Expectation	World

Selected Discography

The Royal Liverpool Philharmonic Orchestra made its first recording (as the Liverpool Philharmonic Orchestra) in January 1943. Lack of space prevents us from listing here all of the recordings that the orchestra has made since. However, this selected discography shows the breadth of the orchestra's recordings. Record labels delete and reissue recordings on a regular basis, so we are unable to guarantee that all of these recordings will be available to buy at any given moment; however with increasing moves to make classical back catalogues available for download, it is quite possible to envisage a time in the future when the RLPO's full library of recordings is available for everyone to own.

COMPILATIONS – ORCHESTRAL
alphabetically by title or first named composer

Bruch Violin Concerto No. 1; **Brahms** Violin Concerto
Vernon Handley conductor, **Tasmin Little** violin
EMI 5749412

Elgar Violin Concerto; **Chausson** Poème
(Original Manuscript Versions)
Vernon Handley conductor, **Philippe Graffin** violin
Avie AV2091

Fleishman / Shostakovich Rothschild's Violin; **Shostakovich** The Gamblers
Vasily Petrenko, Conductor
Avie AV2121

From Jewish Life
Ernest Bloch Schelemo – Hebraic Rhapsody for cello and large orchestra; **Prayer** – from the suite From Jewish Life for cello and strings; **David Diamond** Kaddish for cello and orchestra; **Gerard Schwarz** In Memoriam for cello and string Orchestra; **Max Bruch** Kol Nidrei
Gerard Schwarz conductor, **Jonathan Aasgaard** cello
Avie AV2149

Glinka Russlan and Ludmilla; **Mussorgsky** Night on a Bare Mountain; **Rimsky-Korsakov** Scheherezade; **Shostakovich** Galop
Petr Altrichter conductor, **Malcolm Stewart** violin
RLPO Live RLCD101

Great Movie Themes
Carl Davis conductor, **Thelma Handy** violin
Naxos 8.570505

Heritage and Legacy – Volume 1:
Austin The Sea Venturers; **Elgar** Enigma Variations; **Mackenzie** Prelude to Colomba; **Stanford** Shamus O'Brien; **Vaughan Williams** Fantasia on a Theme of Thomas Tallis
Douglas Bostock conductor
RLPO Live RLCD301

Heritage and Legacy – Volume 2: Elgar – His Forebears and Successors:
Elgar In the South (Alassio); **MacCunn** The Land of the Mountain and the Flood; **Austin** Symphony in E major (world première recording); **Bliss** Pyanepsion from Colour Symphony (first recording of this version)
Douglas Bostock conductor
RLPO Classico CLASSCD 1501

Libor Pešek's French Collection:
Bizet Carmen Suite; **Fauré** Pavane; **Françaix** L'Horloge de Flore*; **Ibert** Divertissement; **Ravel** Boléro
Libor Pešek conductor, **Jonathan Small** oboe*
RLPO Live RLCD302

Prokofiev Romeo and Juliet; **Rachmaninov** Symphony No. 3
Junichi Hirokami conductor
RLPO Live RLCD304

Respighi Church Windows; Kodály Dances of Galanta; Janáček
Taras Bulba
Petr Altrichter conductor
RLPO Live RLCD203

Shostakovich Cello Concerto No.2; Prokofiev Symphony-
Concerto for cello and orchestra
Gerard Schwarz conductor, **Lynn Harrell** cello
Avie AV2090

Strauss Don Quixote; Tchaikovsky Rococo Variations
Gerard Schwarz conductor, **Lynn Harrell** cello, **David
Greenlees** viola
RLPO Live RLCD403

COMPILATIONS – CHORAL AND VOCAL

alphabetically by title or first named composer

Carl Davis' Summer Pops Album
Carl Davis conductor, **Mary Hegarty** soprano, **Bonaventura
Bottone** tenor, **Rhos Male Voice Choir** directed by **Tudor Jones**
RLPO Live RLCD103

Cathedral Classics
Bach Wachet auf; **Berlioz** Shepherd's Farewell; **Butterworth**
Banks of Green Willow; **Clarke** Trumpet Voluntary; **Franck** Panis
Angelicus; **Handel** Hallelujah Chorus and Water Music; **Haydn**
The Heavens are Telling; **Monteverdi** Cantate Domino; **Pachelbel**
Canon; **Parry** I Was Glad; **Vaughan Williams** O Clap Your Hands;
Vivaldi Gloria and Largo; **Walford Davies** God be in my head
Ian Tracey conductor, **Royal Liverpool Philharmonic Choir**
RLPO Live RLCD102

Christmas Carols from the Liverpool Phil
Ian Tracey conductor, **Liverpool Philharmonic Youth Choir**
directed by **Simon Emery**, **Royal Liverpool Philharmonic Choir**
RLPO Live RLCD251

Willard White – A Gala Celebration
Bizet Pearl Fishers Duet ; **Copland** Five Old American Songs ;
Davis On the Beach at Night Alone, Three Spirituals
Carl Davis conductor, **Willard White** bass-baritone,
Bonaventura Bottone tenor, **Royal Liverpool Philharmonic Choir**
RLPO Live RLCD204

BY COMPOSER

alphabetically

Alwyn Concerto for Oboe, Harp and Strings; Elizabethan
Dances; The Innumerable Dance
David Lloyd-Jones conductor, **Jonathan Small** oboe, **Eleanor
Hudson** harp
Naxos 8.570144

Alwyn Concerto grosso No. 1; Pastoral Fantasia; 5 Preludes;
Autumn Legend
David Lloyd-Jones conductor, **Philip Dukes** viola, **Rachael
Pankhurst** cor anglais
Naxos 8.570704

Alwyn Symphonies Nos. 1 and 3
David Lloyd-Jones conductor
Naxos 8.557648

Alwyn Symphonies Nos. 2 and 5; Harp Concerto 'Lyra
Angelica'
David Lloyd-Jones conductor, **Suzanne Willison** harp
Naxos 8.557647

Alwyn Symphony No. 4; Sinfonietta
David Lloyd-Jones conductor
Naxos 8.557649

Sir Malcolm Arnold: An 80th Birthday Tribute
Overture – Beckus the Dandipratt; English Dances, Set 2; The
Sound Barrier Rhapsody; Concerto for Two Pianos (Three
Hands); Symphony No. 2
Douglas Bostock conductor, **Martin Roscoe** piano, **Antonio
Piricone** piano
RLPO Live RLCD402P

Beethoven Symphonies No. 1 and No. 3 'Eroica'
Charles Mackerras conductor
EMI CDEMX 2246

Beethoven Symphonies No. 2 and No. 8
Charles Mackerras conductor
EMI CD CFP 6068

Beethoven Symphonies No. 4 and No. 6 'Pastoral'
Charles Mackerras conductor
EMI CDEMX 2245

Beethoven Symphonies No. 5 and No. 7
Charles Mackerras conductor
EMI CDEMX 2212

Beethoven Symphony No. 9 'Choral'
Charles Mackerras conductor, **Joan Rodgers** soprano, **Della Jones** contralto, **Peter Bronder** tenor, **Bryn Terfel** bass, **Royal Liverpool Philharmonic Choir**
EMI CDEMX 2186

Beethoven Complete Symphonies
Charles Mackerras conductor, **Joan Rodgers** soprano, **Della Jones** contralto, **Peter Bronder** tenor, **Bryn Terfel** bass, **Royal Liverpool Philharmonic Choir**
EMI 575 7512

Bernstein Symphony No. 3 'Kaddish'; Chichester Psalms
Gerard Schwarz conductor, **Yvonne Kenny** soprano, **Willard White** speaker, **Liverpool Metropolitan Cathedral Choir**, **Liverpool Philharmonic Youth Choir**, **Royal Liverpool Philharmonic Choir**
Naxos 8.559456

Britten Four Sea Interludes; Sinfonia da Requiem; Young Person's Guide to the Orchestra
Libor Pešek conductor
Virgin VB 5618352

Brouwer Aurolucent Circles; Mandala; Remembrances
Gerard Schwarz conductor, **Evelyn Glennie** percussion
Naxos 8.559250

Eric Coates By a Sleepy Lagoon; London Suite; The Three Elizabeths
Charles Groves conductor
2 CDs EMI CDCFPD 4456

Eric Coates Concert waltz: Footlights; The Three Men Suite; The Selfish Giant; London Again Suite for Orchestra; Cinderella – A Phantasy; Summer Days Suite; Television March
John Wilson conductor
Avie AV2070

Carl Davis Ben Hur
Carl Davis conductor
Silva Screen FILMCD 043

Frederick Delius in Norway
On the Mountains; Paa Vidderne; Seven Songs; Norwegian Bridal Procession
Douglas Bostock conductor, **Peter Hall** narrator, **Jan Lund** tenor
Classico CLASSCD 364

Delius Cello Concerto; Violin and Cello Concerto; Paris, the Song of a Great City
Charles Mackerras conductor, **Raphael Wallfisch** cello, **Tasmin Little** violin
EMI CDEMX 2185

Elgar Dream of Gerontius; Organ Sonata, orch. Gordon Jacob
Vernon Handley conductor, **Anthony Rolfe-Johnson** tenor, **Catherine Wyn-Rogers** mezzo soprano, **Michael George** bass, **Royal Liverpool Philharmonic Choir**, **Huddersfield Choral Society**
2 CDs EMI CDEMXD 2500

Elgar Dream of Gerontius; Cello Concerto*
Malcolm Sargent conductor, **Heddle Nash** tenor, **Gladys Ripley** contralto, **Dennis Noble** baritone, **Norman Walker** bass, **Huddersfield Choral Society**
Paul Tortelier cello*, BBCSO*
2 CDs Testament SBT 2025

Elgar The Light of Life
Charles Groves conductor, **Margaret Marshall** soprano, **Helen Watts** contralto, **Robin Leggate** tenor, **John Shirley-Quirk** bass, **Royal Liverpool Philharmonic Choir**
EMI CDM 7647322

Elgar – Orchestral Works
Severn Suite; Nursery Suite; Crown of India; Grania and Diarmid; 'Lux Christi' from The Light of Life; Caractacus
Charles Groves conductor
British Composers CDZ5752942

Finzi Intimations of Immortality; Grand Fantasia and Toccata
Richard Hickox conductor, **Philip Fowke** piano, **Philip Langridge** tenor, **Royal Liverpool Philharmonic Choir**
EMI CDM 7647202

Frankel Curse of the Werewolf; The Prisoner; So Long at the Fair Medley
Carl Davis conductor
Naxos 8.557850

Philip Glass The Concerto Project – Vol. 1
Gerard Schwarz conductor, Julian Lloyd-Webber cello, Evelyn
Glennie and Jonathan Haas, timpani
Orange Mountain Music OMM0014

Richard Gordon-Smith Lowlands Away*; Hotfoot on Hope
Street; Overture NOW!
Roy Goodman* conductor, Vernon Handley conductor, Claron
McFadden soprano*, Martyn Hill tenor*, Royal Liverpool
Philharmonic Choir*
RLPO Live RLCD303

Handel Messiah
Malcolm Sargent conductor, Elsie Morrison soprano, Marjorie
Thomas contralto, Richard Lewis tenor, James Milligan bass,
Huddersfield Choral Society
2 CDs Dutton 2CDEA 5010

Hovhaness Mysterious Mountains
Gerard Schwarz conductor
Telarc CD-80604

Howells – Orchestral Works
Concerto for String Orchestra; Three Dances*; Piano Concerto
No. 2
Vernon Handley conductor, Kathryn Stott piano, Malcolm
Stewart violin*
Hyperion CDA66610

Howells – Choral Works
An English Mass; Hymnus Paradisi
Vernon Handley conductor, Julie Kennard soprano, John Mark
Ainsley tenor, Royal Liverpool Philharmonic Choir
Hyperion CDA66488

Lord Durham Concerto
Mischa Damev conductor, Matthew Barley cello, Jon Lord
Hammond organ, Ruth Palmer violin, Kathryn Tickell
Northumbrian pipes
Avie AV2145

Mahler Symphony No. 1
Charles Mackerras conductor
EMI 573 5102

Mahler Symphony No. 1
Gerard Schwarz conductor
Classico CLASSCD 1503

Mahler Symphony No. 4
Gerard Schwarz conductor, Rosa Mannion soprano
Classico CLASSCD 1601

Mahler Symphony No. 5
Charles Mackerras conductor
EMI CDEMX 2164

Mahler Symphony No. 7
Gerard Schwarz conductor
Artek CD 43

McCartney Liverpool Oratorio – highlights
Carl Davis conductor, Kiri Te Kanawa soprano, Sally Burgess
mezzo soprano, Jerry Hadley tenor, Willard White bass-
baritone, Royal Liverpool Philharmonic Choir
EMI CDC 7546422

Mozart Clarinet Concerto; Clarinet Quintet; Adagio in C major
K580a
Roy Goodman conductor, Nicholas Cox basset clarinet
Classico CLASSCD 1502

The Carl Nielsen Edition 1
Symphonies No. 2 and No. 5
Douglas Bostock conductor
Classico CLASSCD 296

The Carl Nielsen Edition 2
Symphony No. 3; Helios Overture; Songs
Douglas Bostock conductor, Eva Hess-Thaysen soprano, Jan
Lund tenor
Classico CLASSCD 297

The Carl Nielsen Edition 3
Symphony No. 4; Cupid and the Poet; Symphonic Rhapsody;
Songs
Douglas Bostock conductor, Jan Lund tenor
Classico CLASSCD 298

The Carl Nielsen Edition 4
Symphonies No. 1 and No. 6 'Sinfonia Semplice'; Andante
Tranquillo e Scherzo
Douglas Bostock conductor
Classico CLASSCD 299

Novák Eternal Longing; In the Tatra Mountains; Slovak Suite
Libor Pešek conductor
Virgin VC 5452512

Prokofiev Romeo and Juliet – highlights
Libor Pešek conductor
Virgin VC 5452512

Rorem Violin Concerto; Flute Concerto; Pilgrims
José Serebrier conductor, Philippe Quint violin, Jeffrey
Khaner flute
Naxos 8.559278

Shostakovich Symphony No. 13 'Babi Yar'
Gerard Schwarz conductor, Gidon Saks bass, Royal Liverpool
Philharmonic Choir
Avie AV2096

Smetana Má Vlast
Libor Pešek conductor
Virgin CUV 561 2232

Richard Strauss Symphonia Domestica; Oboe Concerto; An
Alpine Symphony; Duett-Concertino for clarinet, bassoon and
strings
Gerard Schwarz conductor, Nicholas Cox clarinet, Alan
Pendlebury bassoon
Avie AV2071

Suk Ripening; Praga
Libor Pešek conductor
Virgin VC 7593182

Suk A Summer's Tale
Libor Pešek conductor
Virgin VC 5450572

Sullivan Pineapple Poll (arranged Charles Mackerras);
Symphony in E major 'Irish'
David Lloyd-Jones conductor
Naxos 8.570351

Tchaikovsky 1812 Overture; Marche Slave; Romeo and Juliet
– Fantasy Overture; Francesca da Rimini
Sian Edwards conductor
EMI CDEMX 2152

Tchaikovsky Ballet Music: excerpts from Swan Lake, The
Sleeping Beauty and The Nutcracker
Vasily Petrenko conductor
Avie AV2139

Vaughan Williams Complete Symphonies; English Folk Song
Suite; Fantasia on Greensleeves; Five Variants of Dives and
Lazarus; Flos Campi; Job†; Oboe Concerto*; Partita; Serenade
to Music
Vernon Handley conductor, Jonathan Small oboe*, Royal
Liverpool Philharmonic Choir, LPO †
EMI 575 7602

Vaughan Williams Symphony No. 1 'A Sea Symphony'
Vernon Handley conductor, Joan Rodgers soprano, William
Shimell baritone, Royal Liverpool Philharmonic Choir
EMI CDEMX 2142

Vaughan Williams Symphonies No. 2 'A London Symphony'
and No. 8
Vernon Handley conductor
EMI CDEMX 2209

Vaughan Williams Symphonies No. 3 'Pastoral' and No. 4;
English Folk Song Suite
Vernon Handley conductor, Heather Harper soprano
EMI CDEMX 2192

Vaughan Williams Symphony No. 5; Flos Campi – Suite; Oboe
Concerto
Vernon Handley conductor, Jonathan Small oboe
EMI CDEMX 9512

Vaughan Williams Symphonies No. 6 and No. 9; Fantasia on
Greensleeves
Vernon Handley conductor
EMI CDEMX 2230

Vaughan Williams: Symphony No. 7 'Sinfonia Antarctica';
Serenade to Music; Partita
Vernon Handley conductor, Alison Hargan soprano, RLPC
EMI CDEMX 2173

Vaughan Williams Willow-Wood; The Sons of Light; Toward
the Unknown Region
David Lloyd Jones conductor, Roderick Williams baritone,
Royal Liverpool Philharmonic Choir
Naxos 8.557798

Walton Crown Imperial; Orb and Sceptre; Spitfire Prelude and
Fugue
Charles Groves conductor
EMI CDM 7633692

International Tours

Royal Liverpool Philharmonic Orchestra has represented

the UK on the following foreign tours:

October 1966 **Switzerland and Germany**	Tour of Switzerland and Germany Charles Groves conductor
October 1968 **Germany, Switzerland, Holland**	Tour of Germany, Switzerland and Holland Charles Groves conductor
September 1970 **Poland**	Tour of Poland Charles Groves conductor
October 1973 **France and Luxembourg**	Tour of France and Luxembourg Sir Charles Groves conductor
April 1975 **Holland and Belgium**	Tour of Holland and Belgium Sir Charles Groves conductor
July to August 1979 **Yugoslavia and Austria**	Tour of Yugoslavia and Austria Walter Weller conductor
June 1980 **Germany**	Passau Festival Walter Weller conductor
March to April 1981 **Germany**	Tour of Germany David Atherton conductor
July 1993 **Ireland**	Concerts in Dublin Marek Janowski conductor
April 1986 **Germany**	Tour of Germany Sir Charles Mackerras conductor
October 1988 **Czechoslovakia**	Tour of Czechoslovakia including concerts in Prague, Bratislava and Brno. Libor Pešek conductor
July 1989 **Turkey**	Istanbul Festival
July 1989 **Netherlands**	Kerkrade Festival (The Netherlands)
March / April 1990 **Switzerland**	Tour of Switzerland
October 1990 **Germany**	Performed Mahler's Symphony No.9 in Mannheim, Germany. Libor Pešek conductor
November 1991 **USA**	Concert in Carnegie Hall, New York, of Paul McCartney's Liverpool Oratorio with Carl Davis.

January 1992 **The Canaries**	Tour of the Canaries including concerts in Las Palmas and Puerto de la Cruz. Libor Pešek conductor
February 1992 **USA**	Tour of the USA East Coast, including concerts in Washington (Kennedy Center), around North and South Carolina, Michigan, Boston Symphony Hall, and at the Avery Fisher Hall at the Lincoln Center, New York. Libor Pešek conductor
May 1992 **Spain**	Tour of Spain including 6 performances of Mahler's Symphony No.8 with the Royal Liverpool Philharmonic Choir (Santiago de Compostella, Oviedo, Madrid, Valencia, Barcelona, Seville) Libor Pešek conductor
	Three concerts at the Expo'92 site in Seville, each in the presence of H.R.H. The Prince and Princess of Wales.
November 1992 **France**	Lille Festival (France) performing Paul McCartney's Liverpool Oratorio with the Royal Liverpool Philharmonic Choir.
May 1993 **Czech Republic**	Prague Spring Festival, including the opening concert given for the first time by a non-Czech Orchestra. Libor Pešek conductor
June 1994 **Singapore & Taiwan**	Far East Tour with concerts at the Singapore Arts Festival and in the National Concert Hall, Taipei (Taiwan) Libor Pešek conductor
August 1994 **Spain**	San Sebastian Festival (Spain)
September / October 1994 **Austria & Germany**	A two week tour of Austria and Germany including concerts in Salzburg, Linz, Vienna, Hamburg, Frankfurt and 7 other German towns. Libor Pešek, Adrian Leaper conductors
June 1995 **Germany**	Saarland Festival, Germany: two concerts in Saarbrucken including Tippett's A Child of our Time with the composer present, and Elgar's Dream of Gerontius with the Royal Liverpool Philharmonic Choir.
February 1996 **USA**	Tour of the East Coast of USA (28 day tour) including concerts in Florida, Alabama, North and South Carolina, Virginia and New York states, including a concert at the Avery Fisher Hall, Lincoln Center, New York.
May 1996 **Czech Republic**	Prague Spring Festival (Czech Republic) Ostrava Festival (Czech Republic) Libor Pešek, Petr Altrichter conductors

October 1996 **Slovak Republic** **Austria** **Czech Republic**	Three country tour (in three days) Bratislava Music Festival (Slovak Republic), British Music Festival at the Musikverein, Vienna (Austria) Brno Festival (Czech Republic)
July 1997 **Netherlands**	Kerkrade Festival Rodahal, Kerkrade with RLPC
April 1998 **Switzerland**	Switzerland 7 day tour (6 concerts) with Carl Davis
May 2000 **Czech Republic**	Prague Spring Festival (Czech Republic) Ostrava Festival (Czech Republic) Libor Pešek, Petr Altrichter conductors
9/10 July 2000 **Netherlands**	Kerkrade Festival, Netherlands 2 concerts with the Royal Liverpool Philharmonic Choir Including Vaughan Williams A Sea Symphony / Vernon Handley and a concert of British music conducted by Douglas Bostock
September 2002 **Czech Republic**	Prague Autumn Festival: opening concert Programme of Suk, Janáček, Martinů and Dvořák Brno Philharmonic Orchestra : opening concert of the season Programme of Mendelssohn, Mozart (Ivan Moravec) and Elgar Libor Pešek, conductor
September / Ocotber 2005 **Czech Republic**	Prague Autumn Festival Janáček Suite, The Cunning Little Vixen; Czech Arias (Jitka Svobodova) and Dvořák Symphony No. 6 Bach-Elgar, Grieg Piano Concerto (Ewa Kupiec) and Holst The Planets Gerard Schwarz conductor
March 2006 **Spain**	Spain: Concerts in Murcia, Valencia, Madrid, Oviedo and Zaragoza. Gerard Schwarz conductor
July 2006 **Malta**	Outdoor Gala at Fort Manoel. Vasily Petrenko conductor
September 2008 **Prague**	Prague Autumn Festival Libor Pešek conductor and Vasily Petrenko conductor
October 2008 **Germany and Holland**	Concerts in Germany and Holland Vasily Petrenko conductor

Royal Liverpool Philharmonic Orchestra

† denotes Honorary Life Member of the Royal Liverpool Philharmonic Society

Principal Conductor
Vasily Petrenko

Conductor Laureate
Libor Pešek KBE

Conductor Emeritus
Vernon Handley CBE (deceased 10th September 2008)
Sir Charles Mackerras CH AC CBE (from January 2009)

Composer in the House
Kenneth Hesketh

Royal Liverpool Philharmonic Choir Chorus Master
Ian Tracey

First Violins
James Clark leader
Thelma Handy leader
Lesley Gwyther †
Martin Richardson
Clifford Bibby †
Alexander Marks
Donald Turnbull †
John Hebbron †
David Whitehead †
Stephan Mayer
Concettina Del Vecchio
Ruth Longmaid

Second Violins
Kate Richardson
Jenny Stokes
Kate Marsden
Martin Anthony Burrage †
James Hutton
Gerald Adamson †
Celia Goodwin
Justin Evans
Sally Anne Thomson
Nicola Gleed

Violas
Robert Shepley †
David Ruby
Richard Wallace †
Fiona Stunden
Joanna Wesling
Rebecca Walters
Rachel Jones
Sarah Hill

Cellos
Jonathan Aasgaard
Hilary Browning
Ian Bracken
Gethyn Jones †
Stephen Mann
Ruth Owens
Alexander Holladay

Double Basses
Marcel Becker
Ashley Frampton
Nigel Dufty
Daniel Hammerton †
Genna Spinks

Flutes
Cormac Henry
Fiona Paterson

Piccolo
Myra Bennett †

Oboes
Jonathan Small
Ruth Davies

Cor Anglais
Rachael Pankhurst

Clarinets
Nicholas Cox
Mandy Burvill

Bass Clarinet
Katherine Lacy

Bassoons
Alan Pendlebury
Sarah Whibley

Contrabassoon
Gareth Twigg

Horns
Simon Griffiths
David Pigott †
Timothy Nicholson
Christopher Morley

Trumpets
Rhys Owens
Paul Marsden
Brendan Ball

Tenor Trombone
Simon Cowen
Blyth Lindsay †

Bass Trombone
Simon Chappell

Tuba
Robin Haggart

Timpani
Neil Hitt

Percussion
Graham Johns †
Josephine Large

Index